WESTON-SUPER-MARE IN WATERCOLOURS

an alternative guide

Rosie and Howard Smith

The Garret Press

First published in the United Kingdom in 2001

The Garret Press, 6, Stafford Place, Weston-super-Mare, Somerset BS23 2QZ.

British Library Cataloguing in Publication Data.

A catalogue record for this book is available from the British Library.

ISBN

0-9541546-0-6 (paperback)

0-9541546-1-4 (hardback)

Cover illustration: Late summer afternoon, Knightstone Harbour.

Design: Colin Baker.

Type: 12 pt. Perpetua.

Printed in Great Britain by: R. Booth Limited, Antron Hill, Mabe, Penryn, Cornwall TR10 9HH.

ACKNOWLEDGEMENTS

We would like to thank Laura and Allan Hoyano, Paul Smith, Kathie Barnes, John Crockford-Hawley and Samuel Smith for their reading and advice on the text. Although we had a definite idea as to how we wanted the book to appear, it was only through the guidance of David Brown and, particularly, our designer Colin Baker that this became a reality.

Through our association with Weston-super-Mare Civic Society we have had many discussions with Bob Smart, Martin Taylor and Philip Beisly about the town and its story. Indeed it was a series of talks given by Bob Smart in the late 1970s which kindled our anxiety about Weston's architectural heritage. These days that legacy does appear to be a little more secure. Chris Richards and Sharon Poole have clarified many areas of uncertainty. Any lack of clarity that remains is our responsibility. Thanks as well to Stan and Joan Rendell for their advice on publishing and information about Steep and Flat Holms.

We are also grateful to Judi Kisiel and David Lawrence for their supportive enthusiasm when we discussed the book with them in its early stages.

This book is dedicated to our parents and to our children.

INTRODUCTION

A SHORT HISTORY

INTRODUCTION

It came as a shock to me to discover that a busy, jolly lady who had spent more than sixty years of her life in Weston, had never visited Anchor Head.

The perception of the town is so locked into the tripper-zone of the sea-front, that much of Weston-super-Mare is left unregarded and undiscovered. There is surely a place for a simple, but communicative guide. The plan here is to deliver information in the main text, with Rosie's watercolours as beguiling tempters. I have also added footnotes and 'Special Pages' with additional details and stories, hoping they might prompt the reader to look further.

Anchor Head

A SHORT HISTORY

In the late 18th century Weston-super-Mare was still a small village tucked into the southern slopes of the seaward end of Worlebury Hill. Its small church and scatter of fishermen's huts looked out over a wide, sweeping bay of hard yellow sand. High dunes protected the marshy plain which lay to the east, with the enclosing promontory of Brean Down to the south. Out in the Channel the islands of Steep Holm and Flat Holm completed a picturesque scene.

As the century closed, visitors from Bristol and Bath, eager to try out the new 'sea bathing,' started to make the difficult journey across the Northmarsh plain beyond Congresbury. Fashionable folk were beginning to tire of the older inland spa resorts, and it had become much more dangerous to visit the Continent since the French Revolution.

Weston-super-Mare 1829 (After John Rutter)

In 1808 the Pigott family (Lords of the Manor since 1696) sold the fishing huts and accompanying land to Richard Parsley and William Cox - Weston's first developers. Two years later, by way of an Act of Parliament, the fishermen were out and the builders were in. By 1812 the town had its first hotel, described at the time as "a large and profitless inn." Imaginatively given the name 'The Hotel,' it later became 'The Royal' and the fishermen's shacks had given way to "a town of commodious and handsome lodging houses." In 1822 the first bath-house was built on Knightstone Island, and in 1824 the small, medieval parish church was demolished and rebuilt. 1841 brought the railway via a branch from the Bristol and Exeter main line. At this time the town was expanding furiously - from 163 residents in 1811 to 2,103 thirty years later. By 1901 it had topped 19,000 and today (the year 2000) it exceeds 70,000.

One of the defining episodes in the town's history was the construction of the New Sea Front. Building began in January 1883 and took three years, with a small hiccup in the October of that first year when a great tidal gale destroyed a quarter mile length of the partially built wall. The sea wall is masonry of great quality - a curving configuration of local stone with ramparts which fuse with the high rocks at Birnbeck, which then bends around the hill to mould itself into Glentworth and Weston Bays, running out to the lower wall following the sand-line south towards Uphill. No other event in the town has quite matched the self-confidence expressed in the completion of that sea wall.

By 1841 Weston had its own Gas Works and in 1853 a public Water Works was established - until then people had had to rely on private springs and wells, and rain water was collected and stored in brick cisterns under their houses. A sophisticated network of sewers was constructed. In 1901 electricity arrived.

For the next 30 years Weston consolidated its position as a seaside resort. Many of the houses which ran back from the seafront were built with an extra room or two to accommodate paying guests during the summer season. Everyone was getting in on the action. A theatre and salt-water swimming baths sprang up on Knightstone Island. The town sported two magnificent piers. Paddle steamers brought visitors from Wales, and trains, trippers from the Midlands. Weston was also seen as an healthy place to educate children, and a large number of private schools opened to care for the offspring of the British Empire's civil servants who lived and worked abroad.

Development stalled with the First World War and only picked up slowly during the 1920s. Despite the Depression, the town found fresh energy in the late 1920s and 1930s with several high quality public projects - a stunning Art Deco swimming pool, the Winter Gardens ballroom and the construction of the tidal barrier across Glentworth Bay to form the Marine Lake. All this optimism was flattened by the Second World War and Weston emerged in 1945 with a badly damaged town centre and a damaged idea of itself. Poor decisions by Weston's Borough Council led to the destruction of some of the town's finest buildings and incoherent planning undermined its character and atmosphere. Being Victorian wasn't cool. Holiday makers left for the Mediterranean and Weston floundered trying to make itself into something it could never be.

In the late 1950s the town began to expand eastwards, consuming the village of Worle in the process, and forming a new distinct district of North Worle. In 1970 the M5 motorway arrived and today, at the turn of the millennium, and against its wishes, Weston is expanding further into the south-east and is set to encircle Locking village. But, at long last, the town is beginning to value and protect its Victorian heritage, and to appreciate what those first visitors saw when they came here - a wonderful seascape and a beguiling environment: a really nice place to live.

Chapter One

THE SEA-FRONT · GRAND PIER AND NORTH SHORE

The promenade, outside the Grand Pier, seems a good place to start. Although there have been many changes, it is easy to understand what brought those early visitors here. Worlebury Hill, Knightstone Island, the easy curve of the bay, all have a satisfying symmetry which can still be seen and enjoyed.

Feet up! On the Promenade

The sea-wall rises some 12 feet from the beach where Trapnell's and Majer's donkeys wait patiently for their young riders. The Grand Pier faces Regent Street in its splendid Art Deco[1] reincarnation. The entrance was remodelled in the 1960s and plies a seaside trade of fish and chips, toffee apples and candy floss. The walk along the pier to the Deco pavilion is a bargain - there is no entrance fee! It was along here that scenes from the film 'Remains of the Day' were shot. Looking back the town acquires a fresh perspective settled comfortably under the hill. Inside the pavilion is all the rowdy

clatter of a funfair. Shrieks from the dodgems, the Crazy House, the Castle of Doom and Dead Man's Cove. The machines Laurie Lee describes in 'Cider with Rosie,' where various condemned men are forever being strung up or garrotted, have moved on - some to Weston Museum. Beyond the pavilion the whole of Weston Bay opens up before you - a magnificent panorama.

Back on the prom, looking across Royal Parade to the buildings facing the beach, we see, what for so many is, Weston-super-Mare. Shops selling 'Kiss-me-quick hats,' chips, sweets, rock, ice-cream, buckets and spades, and more chips - all in a higgledy-piggledy cluster of sand and hot oil. Fella's is the last of many Italian businesses (Forte's especially) which made and sold ice-cream in various 'Parlors' before and after the Second World War. Fella's, which once had several shops and an ice-cream factory, is now just a lone

[1] *The Grand Pier was completed in 1904 and was originally designed to receive paddle steamers, although only three ever called because of the shallow sea. The first theatre pavilion burned down spectacularly in 1930 - my father watched it burn - and was replaced, three years later, by the Art-Deco funfair, which has been the key to its continuous financial success and survival.*

kiosk fronting Victoria Square - a cipher of its former self. The square, once a small garden park, is now home to a Crazy Golf Course and is overlooked by substantial three storey terraced houses divided into flats for holiday letting. The Sovereign Centre's sea-front entrance forms the square's eastern boundary, and the Centre's cafe has a dramatic view of the Grand Pier Pavilion. Maybe, one day, the small park will return.

A few yards north of Victoria Square stands the shallow silver dome of the Winter Gardens' ballroom and behind, its conference centre.[2]

Just beyond the ballroom, the esplanade suddenly opens out to extensive lawns which front the Cabot, Grosvenor and Royal Hotels. Sadly, some of this has been sacrificed to car-parking, but it remains an attractive and uncluttered space, setting off the hotel buildings superbly.[3]

Next to the Cabot Hotel, Knightstone Road joins the promenade and takes over from Royal Parade, curving north-west towards Knightstone Island. Across the road from the Cabot is The Thatched Cottage which has the distinction of being one of Weston's oldest buildings. The cottage was built in 1791 by the Rev. William Leeves of Wrington for his summer holidays.[4]

[2] *The Winter Gardens ballroom together with its Summer Gardens of tennis courts and a putting green were built in 1927. The ballroom remains true to its time with a lowered dance-floor, pastel colours and a circumferential sitting area. In the early 1990s the tennis courts gave way to the Conference Centre extension which houses five large ceramic tile panels by Rosie Smith depicting Weston's parks. The loss of the sheltered rose garden is still mourned.*

[3] *These areas of undeveloped land were a feature of this part of the sea-front until well into the 20th century. They were kept open by restrictive covenants which protected the sea views of various boarding houses. Amongst the last to be built on was the Winter Gardens' site, and even more recently the conference centre extension, which required the agreement of the Royal Hotel to go ahead. A little further around the bay, at Park Place, the open land has been tarmacked into a car-park. Close by, more becomingly, the lawns have been retained as a putting course.*

[4] *Even in 1902 it was considered to be "one of the few remaining relics of Old Weston", although by then it had become Reed's Dairy. It is now the town's sole thatched building and is a genuine link with Weston's genteel past. In Rev. W. Leeves' time the village ended about here, with a rough track going on to Knightstone. It must have been an idyllic spot.*

For many years cream teas were served on a grassy lawn. Nowadays it is a restaurant and the lawn has been paved. However it's here the buildings give us a hint of what the sea-front was like 150 years ago. Looking east down Knightstone Road, before the ten storey Weston College, is the Lauriston Hotel for the

Victoria Buildings, Knightstone Road

Blind. Its fine main building is late Victorian but the house which forms an annex to the hotel is much earlier. Moving past Leeves' cottage and around the County Hotel, which abuts the pavement, we come to two more houses, with simple classical proportions, one of which has kept its garden and front lawn. It is easy to imagine deckchairs and lemonade. A glass of Pimm's: some croquet perhaps? These two houses, which are alone in retaining their original frontage, are the last of a terrace called Victoria Buildings built in the 1830s. The present day hotels still retain some of their 19th century character - especially at first floor level - although all have added a third storey and a jumble of sun-lounges.

Immediately north of the first group of hotels is the Melrose car park (named after the former Melrose hotel - now the Old Colonial) with its unfortunate row of tatty garages. This was originally the park that fronted Park Place - the line of large houses occupying the northern boundary. Amongst these, Park House (no.1) and Saville House (no.2) are largely unaltered. The adjacent putting green is a treasure and recaptures the original atmosphere of quiet gentility (pity about the peculiar two storey bradstone shed though). Also overlooking this ex-parkland is Royal Crescent which, with its Georgian proportions and bathstone facing, aspires to grander things. Built in the late 1840s Royal Crescent, for years semi-abandoned, is at last undergoing a sympathetic restoration.

The western boundary of Park Place is formed by the narrow road Greenfield Place, most of which is occupied by Greenfield Terrace, rather more exuberantly Victorian than Royal Crescent. Greenfield Place leads to Upper Church Road, filled on its south side with a terrace of small hotels. In summer, their basement front gardens are chockfull with flowers and hanging baskets. There is an atmosphere of friendly competition, reinforced by the Criterion and Raglan Arms pubs, facing one another across the narrow street. There is a real English seaside holiday atmosphere on offer here! Behind Greenfield Place is another redundant garden-park (now Hampton car park) which served the guest houses which back onto it. It's not so long ago that there were tennis courts here. It's good that the area has been well restored with substantial iron railings and stone walls.

Back on the sea-front, and beyond Greenfield Place, is another terrace of hotels echoing the pattern of Victoria Buildings, but this time named after Queen Victoria's husband Albert. The terrace ends at Knightstone causeway which leads to Knightstone Island. On the island stand Dr. Fox's Bath-house, the Theatre Pavilion and Baths. Viewed from the esplanade these buildings form a dramatic group. Indeed, along with the Grand Pier, they are part of the town's inimitable identity.

Dr. Fox's Bath-house, Knightstone Island

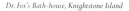

The Marine Lake Causeway

Despite their importance to Weston's seaside scene, these buildings have an uncertain future and have been allowed to become semi-derelict. Dr. Fox's has been externally restored however, and its well-looking appearance underlines what its two companions cry out for. In their prime the baths were salt-water. Sea water was cleared in huge settling tanks under the baths. They were a swimmer's delight and floating was no problem! The island remains a popular spot for local fishermen and in recent years the paddle-ship Waverley has managed to dock at Knightstone[5] - when a big spring tide has cooperated. There are splendid views from the most westerly side of the island and this is probably the best spot to get an all-in perspective of Weston Bay.

[5] *It was supposed that the name Knightstone derived from the island having been the burial place of a Roman knight. When 'human bones of gigantic size' were discovered during early building work this seemed to confirm the tradition. Unfortunately they were carried off by 'a man from Bristol.' So the story's just a bit unreliable. In 1822 the first open-air baths were opened together with various hot and cold sea-water treatments. People even drank the stuff! In about 1830 Dr.Long Fox of Brislington bought the island and converted the pebbly path, which then linked it to the mainland, into a causeway. He built the handsome bath-house (which still stands) and lodging houses which later made way for the theatre and the baths in the early 1900s. The construction of the causeway also meant that, for the first time, ships could anchor with some shelter in Weston Bay.*

Returning to the shore, at the Upper Church Road junction with the promenade, Knightstone Road becomes Birnbeck Road. The three storey terrace facing Marine Lake used to be called Prince's Buildings.[6] It was erected in the 1840s and has survived pretty well unchanged with a simple frontage of classical proportions. Most of the houses have been converted into flats. Prince's Buildings originally ended at Glentworth Hall, a fine house with curved gables and bay windows. One of the saddest casualties of 1970 modernisation, its substitute blocks of flats are, to say the least, a heavy handed intrusion. The Marine Lake and its sea retaining causeway were part of a 1920/30s push to develop Weston's tourist attractions. This area had always been known as Glentworth Bay and to some it still is.

Sea Dogs

The Marine Lake was an attempt to solve the disappearing sea problem by trapping the tide within a barrier thrown across the small bay from Knightstone to the esplanade below Claremont Crescent. The scheme also involved the promenade being extended beyond the Victorian sea-wall to provide changing rooms below with shelters, ticket booths and ice-cream stalls above. There was one very high slide which, dangerously, shot you out into deep water. There were pontoons to swim out to and a variety of boats to mess about in. However the lake needed (and still does) regular dredging to avoid silting, and when the local council largely abandoned its responsibility in 1970/80 - it silted up completely! In 1981 an enormous tidal storm rearranged things by smashing the promenade extension. It then had to be demolished and the Victorian sea wall repaired and restored. The tidal barrier/causeway survived, so the Marine Lake is still a place where children can have sea and sand all day long. The high encircling stone wall is wonderfully sheltering and this area of the beach is a great sun-trap.

[6]The building on the west corner of Upper Church Road, directly opposite Knightstone causeway, was formerly 'Forte's No.2 Ice-cream Parlor'- they used the American spelling. It was one of three Fortes establishments in the town run by various members of the same Italian family. Immediately behind the parlour was an ice-cream factory. It made the ice-cream for the other Fortes in the town and surrounding area. Many who remember the ice-cream rate it the "best ever." Firm, icy crystals, creamy, not too sweet. Perfection. Even during the war, Fortes continued to make ice-cream "for the National Morale." When supplies of pineapple dried up, Fortes No.2 designed a replacement with turnip chips and pineapple essence. After the war, when real pineapples returned, people complained about the change in flavour! Nancy Browns, Eskimo Pies, North Poles, Knickerbocker Glories, Fresh Fruit Sundaes... their coffee and ring doughnuts were pretty good too. There are still Fortes to be found in Clevedon and Burnham-on-Sea.

The Hillside, from Knightstone

Beyond Knightstone, Weston-super-Mare's character changes. The town takes on a quieter, more reflective mood. Grand terraces form up on the hillside. Holy Trinity church spire breaks the skyline like an exclamation mark. The woods are close by and soften the line of Worlebury Hill. Along the promenade is the convex curve of Claremont Crescent.[7] You can stop off at Dauncey's Hotel for a drink on their veranda to view the sea stretching the whole way to Brean Down and beyond. It is a great place on a summer evening. Below the crescent, the promenade follows the line of the promontory, and then narrows as the sea-front buildings crowd in, jostling for position. This is Anchor Head.[8] A small pebbled cove with great rocks for climbing and the sea close at hand. Don't tell anyone! You can stretch out on the warm sloping stone while children fish for crabs from the old slipway. A restorative, from all this exhausting activity, is close by in the cafes tucked up above and behind the sea-wall. The jetty at Anchor Head gives fishing and excursion boats a choice of landing place besides Knightstone. It has the advantage of boats being able to come and go at almost all states of the tide, but it desperately needs to be properly maintained.

As we continue around Anchor Head the sea-wall rises on rocky cliffs as the promenade constricts to a path around the footings of the Royal Pier Hotel. Steps lead upwards and suddenly the promenade opens out again, with the vista of Birnbeck Pier (the Old Pier) on Birnbeck Island. This is one of the most dramatic moments along Weston's shoreline with the elegant cast-iron pier reaching out from the hillside to the pierhead buildings on the island and Sand Bay beyond.

[7] *The pineapples which adorn the doorways on the landward side of Claremont Crescent were made at Weston's Royal Potteries. See the 'Special Page'.*

[8] *In 1820 Anchor Head was regarded as "the bathing place appropriated exclusively to the ladies. Gentlemen are considered as intruders and will do well to avoid exciting the indignation of the priestess of the retreat..." The latter being one formidable Betty Mugglesworth. Despite the slipway, Weston's tidal waters are pretty shallow for much of the time and for this reason the Weston Flatner was devised - a flat-bottomed boat which could cope with most conditions. I can still remember when fishing was an important local industry with nets hanging out to dry along the railings of Knightstone causeway. The nets were staked out at Anchor Head and Birnbeck becoming submerged at high tide. A great variety of fish were caught including cod, haddock and salmon. In season sprats (a sort of very small herring) were caught in great numbers and served deliciously fried with bread and butter.*

Approaching the Old Pier, beyond Anchor Head

Not surprising then that it was chosen by the BBC as the setting in Pride and Prejudice where Darcy catches the dastardly Wickham with his sister. Mind you, you can't see the pier - but you can see Steep Holm - and it's supposed to be Ramsgate! Above Birnbeck, on low cliffs, sits Prince Consort Gardens. The steps march up from the road opposite the Royal Pier Hotel and from the top lawns, the whole of Weston Bay comes back into view.

The Refreshment Buffet
at the entrance to The Old Pier

The Old Pier on Birnbeck Island

Birnbeck Pier was designed and constructed by the master pier-builder Eugenius Birch in 1867. The main structure is of cast-iron with wrought iron being used for the tie bars, the whole configuration an engineering masterpiece for its day. At first, boat excursions from the pier to Minehead and Wales were organised on a rather ad hoc basis. From 1893 Campbells ran steamers from Weston to Cardiff and beyond, eventually becoming the White Funnel fleet. Indeed Weston, or rather Birnbeck, became such a popular destination for Welsh visitors that many got no further than the pubs on the island! For many years a fully fledged fun-fair was established on the island with some pretty formidable rides. Campbells continued successfully until well after the second world war but by 1970 the arrival of the motorway and the Severn Bridge saw business fall away. In 1972 Campbells sold up and in 1979 the steamship Balmoral made its last call. From that time the pier became increasingly dilapidated as various owners failed to make it work economically. The present owners have made a good start with the restoration of the refreshment buffet, but they face a daunting task.

The pier continues to be the home of the Weston Lifeboat - the lifeboat house on the south side of the island has a famously long slipway and used to be a favourite place to visit. The state of the pier decking means this is no longer possible. Maybe again one day. We still hear the bangs of the exploding maroons which summon the lifeboatmen to their station. Not so often nowadays, as bleeps and mobile phones take over. Which is a shame, because the detonations somehow involve you in the drama taking place in the Channel.

Chapter Two

Donkeys at the Grand Pier

Close by the south side of the Grand Pier entrance stand two stacks of council deckchairs. These are the lonely remainders of chairs the council used to let out, up and down the whole length of the promenade. Working on the chairs was a popular student job during the long vacation. It is still fondly recalled, a bit like Forte's ice-cream. The perfect summer job! This is the area with which the town is traditionally identified. In high season and sunny weather it encapsulates the British sea-side holiday. A delicious combination of chips and vinegar mixing with the ozone. There's a bustle up and down Regent Street: amusement arcades, pubs, cafes and restaurants, sweet shops and souvenir shops. A drift of sand underfoot.

The Perfect Summer Job

You had to be well organised to get the deck-chair jobs - or have contacts....
I worked the Grand Pier Stack, which was almost hard work, but friends, sitting in lone booths
in remote regions of the prom, could watch whole mornings drift by without hiring out a chair.
Trouble was, you could be sacked for falling asleep - on a warm dozey afternoon that
could be a bit difficult to avoid.

We had blue jackets with 'Deck Chairs' in red and yellow on the breast pocket - these became
collectors' items. Because the sun always shone in those days and 1960s sun cream was pretty
ineffective, I wore a lint patch to protect my nose which attracted a lot of Brummie banter.
A friend of mine wore aluminium foil. He also had a huge khaki cotton coat (they had run out of
blue jackets), dark glasses and a straw hat. His mother, sitting on the Sand Bay bus, refused to
acknowledge him as her own when he tapped on her window. She needn't have worried,
a few days later he was caught fast asleep.

At the Grand Pier Stack, if it did just happen to rain, everyone would pour off the beach and
demand their deposit. Thousands. All at the same time. The promenade would be littered with
abandoned chairs and windbreaks. It was a bit hectic for a while and afterwards you could be
pretty sure the rest of the day would be quiet. But it could be very tiring staying awake.

The fountain on the raised area of the Beach Lawns is splashing away and people are stretched out on the grass. There is a friendly busyness about and the wide promenade allows you to move freely despite the crowds. Even the occasional roller-skater/roller-blader can whizz by.

And here comes the train! The warm sugary smell of candy-floss. Children shrieking as their donkeys canter back to base. With a bit of luck the tide will be in, sneaking under the pier when you weren't looking. The sea is warm. Walk out a bit and the soft mud will squeeze deliciously between your toes.

If you've worked up a bit of an appetite get a 'worth of cockles or whelks' at the seafood beach stall. With pepper and vinegar they are as good as ever. Sit on the sea-wall and let your fingers explore the extraordinary honeycomb weathering of the capping stones. If you're lucky Punch and Judy might show up. What more can you ask.

Weathered sea-wall capping stones

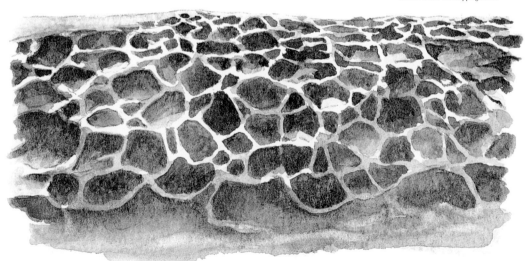

At the top of Regent Street the Beach Lawns begin. The Lawns are a Weston institution which always seem to be under threat, but at the same time are jealously guarded and watched over. Despite the raised beds and the Information Centre, they sweep splendidly southwards with the eye satisfyingly coming to rest at the Holm oaks of the putting green and the chateau towers of the Royal Sands.[9]

To east and west the Beach Lawns are bounded by Beach Road and Marine Parade respectively. A high protective rockery runs for more than half the length of the Lawns and divides them from Marine Parade and the beach. Without the rockery, sand drift would be almost impossible to control and the grass would revert to dunes. As it is, you can walk and sit in perfect comfort out of the keen west wind. For it must be avowed, Weston is often windy!

From Regent Street to Carlton Street, for 200 yards or so, the landward side of Beach Road is unpleasant. The 1930s buildings of the old Grand Central Hotel and Forte's No.1 (now a pub and a club) are in reasonable shape. However, further on is little more than a messy clutter of half-finished buildings, open sites and incomplete developments. This critical part of the sea-front is crying out for clear design guidance. Unfortunately, in the past councillors have not followed their own planning guidelines. For example, the old Woodspring District Council allowed the brown brick affront of Carlton Mansions[10] to rise 2 storeys above the agreed 5 storey ceiling for the sea-front. This has resulted in one of Weston's finest buildings - the Grand Atlantic Hotel - appearing overpowered and hemmed in.

[9]*Completed in 1868 and originally called the Royal West of England Hospital it was known to locals as the Sanatorium or 'the San.' It was designed for the treatment of chronic debilitating illnesses such as tuberculosis. Weston was considered to have 'a climate second to no seaside town in England' for such curative regimes and comparative life-span charts were often shown. With the arrival of the NHS in 1948, it became part of the acute medical care in the town, closing in 1985 when the new general hospital was built at Uphill. With new building, it now forms a group of apartments and houses.*

[10]*Woodspring also messed up by allowing Carlton Mansions to be developed on the site of a much missed and still needed bus station. The original 'Beach Garage and Bus Station' was a handsome 1930s building.*

The Royal Potteries

Sitting on an alluvial plain, with the accumulated mud from the Severn Estuary, Weston had a ready supply of good quality clay. As soon as the town began to grow, a number of small brickyards were established, first in Uphill, and later on in Weston. Brickmakers were recruited from areas like Bridgwater where bricks and tiles had been manufactured for many years.

In 1847 Charles Phillips bought the Weston-super-Mare Pottery in Locking Road from William Wilcox and almost immediately expanded the business, designing a huge range of garden pots, statues, urns and vases. In 1851 his pots gained an Honourable Mention at the Great Exhibition and soon after Phillips had renamed his business 'The Phillips' Royal Potteries.' By this time he was supplying the Royal Parks and Kew Gardens. Fired Weston clay had a quality that resisted disfiguring algae growth.

The Victorian period was one of active expansion and creativity, although after he sold the Potteries to John Matthews in 1871, Charles Phillips slid into penury and, at the age of 70, ended up as caretaker of a promenade cloakroom, opposite the Grand Atlantic Hotel.

During the 1890s, the Potteries moved to a new site with fresh clay pits. This was positioned at the southern end of what is now Langford Road, where some of the brick sheds are still standing. At its height the business employed nearly 150 people and continued, through various crises, up to 1961 when its fate was sealed by the introduction of the plastic flower pot.

Innumerable Royal Potteries' products still survive - the pineapples above the doorways in Claremont Crescent, the White Lion in St. James Street, terracotta copings on stone walls and many treasured pots and urns in homes and gardens about Weston and beyond. Apparently, there are still some pots to be found at Kew Gardens.

Despite its neighbours, the Grand Atlantic[11] still manages to have a strong architectural presence on the sea-front. This, Weston's only example of a European grand hotel - itself cleverly extended in the 19th century - is now badly let down by the company it has been forced to keep.

The Grand Atlantic Hotel

50 yards south of the Grand Atlantic we come to the western part of Ellenborough Park. This part is mainly a school playing field. The eastern section has recently been opened to the public. Ellenborough Park, in its entirety, originally provided the sea view vista for the grand homes of Ellenborough Crescent. The Crescent itself, built in the mid 1850s, is faced in bathstone and, like Royal Crescent, looks to the terraces of Bath for its inspiration.

[11] *Originally built as a school called Atlantic College in 1854, it was converted into a hotel in 1889. An early advertisement describes; "Pure air, direct Atlantic breezes, an inexhaustible supply of water and a rate of mortality of 9.6 per 1,000"!*

Ellenborough Crescent

Back on the beach, facing Ellenborough Park (and blocking the view), is the Sea Life Centre. In some ways this is Weston's third pier although it barely gets its legs wet. The original concept was for something much grander but, in later plans, the aquarium shrank and the shops and cafes enlarged. Further south, down the promenade, lies another of the town's Big Problems. The Tropicana. Up until 1984, this was a superb Art Deco swimming pool. Called simply 'The Pool,'[12] it boasted a magnificent 13 metre diving stage and a large sea-water swimming area. With its conversion into the Tropicana, the town lost something that was unique and classy. Weston still cries out for a covered swimming pool on this site.

[12] *The Pool was part of that exciting 1930s development push which saw the building of the Winter Gardens, Marine Lake and the Odeon cinema. As with the Knightstone Baths, the Pool was sea water. The swimming area was large and, just below the high diving stage, deep - 15 feet deep. From the highest diving stage the view of the town was amazing, and the Pool shrank to the size of a postage stamp. It took a lot of courage to jump, let alone dive, from that top stage. I never did. Even from the second stage it was a long way, and after you hit the water you just kept on going down. Forever it seemed. It even got dark - but perhaps I was just losing consciousness. In summer, the height was extended by a further ten feet, so that acrobatic divers could leap after setting themselves on fire. The diving shows were a regular feature during the season.*

The Waverley

About a hundred yards south of the Tropicana is the second of two boating pools sited on the beach. The other is north of the Grand Pier. These large, raised ponds are replenished and refreshed by the tides. Despite the broken glass warnings, they present an overwhelming temptation to reckless paddlers.

From Ellenborough Park the Beach Lawns proceed south and the fine villas, standing to attention along Beach Road, have survived largely intact. These houses keep to themselves, and their stately procession adds to the feeling of spaciousness of the whole bay. Indeed, should you arrive at Beach Road from the south, this sudden opening out of the Lawns is another of the town's surprises. Looking north with the hill as backdrop, westering sunlight reflected from spires and terraces... the islands.... a cargo ship or two.....

Sarah's pebbles

The Beach Lawns, looking South

The processional villas make up the western boundary of Clarence Park which provides a sheltered retreat from the sea-front. Further on, the Beach Lawns have the fitting finale of the Royal Sand's gables and towers. Just beyond lies Weston Golf Course which runs the entire length of Uphill Road North until it meets the small wood[13] which separates Weston from Uphill Village. On the seaward side the golf course is protected by high sand dunes[14] - which at one time ran almost the whole length of the bay, to just beyond where the Grand Pier now stands. Although the promenade ends at the Royal Sands, the seashore continues, with a wide beach, for nearly a mile to the estuary of the River Axe, overlooked by the part-roofless church of St. Nicholas on its "high hill crest."

[13] *This wood was once part of the Uphill Castle / Manor Estate and remains an important boundary between Weston-super-Mare town and Uphill village. It is now owned and managed by the Woodland Trust. The trust has also taken over the adjoining field on Uphill Road South - known in these here parts as the 'donkey field.' It is famous for its spring flowers (bluebells, cowslips).*

[14] *A few years ago the sand-dunes near the clubhouse were tidied up and the buckthorn cut back - with dangerous consequences. Sand blew onto the Links and threatened some of the greens. Replanting and reconstruction of the dunes was achieved only with great difficulty.*

Chapter Three

THE SANDS AND THE SEA AND THE TIDES

Weston Bay is two and a half miles of sand and sea (and a bit of mud) enclosed by the promontories of Worlebury Hill and Brean Down. It is the central of three bays - Sand Bay to the north, bounded by Sand Point and Worlebury, and to the south, Bridgwater Bay which runs from Brean to Burnham-on-Sea and the estuaries of the Rivers Parrett and Brue. All three have superb firm sand where you can play cricket or soccer, ride a horse or a donkey, run a dog, make a sand castle, fly a kite, sail a land yacht..... In Weston, the sand has a curious habit of moving from the north end of the bay down to Uphill (longshore drift) - this may have been aggravated by the sea defences. So, every once in a while, the sand is loaded into lorries and taken back to Knightstone.

Uphill Sands

Weston-super-Mare lies on the Bristol Channel (the Severn Sea) which is the tidal estuary of the river Severn. The tidal range in the estuary is the second highest in the world, beaten only by the Bay of Fundy in eastern Canada. It is also relatively shallow and this explains why the sea does its notorious disappearing act twice a day. It also explains why the Channel was so favoured as a huge hydroelectric generator - the Severn Barrage - which may still have a future, in some form, when the oil runs out.

High Tide at Anchor Head

At the time of the Spring tides[15] (when the rise and fall of water is at its maximum, twice a month) the sea comes in furthest and goes out farthest - almost slipping out of sight over the horizon. But when it is in, on a really high tide (say 14 metres), the Grand Pier and Knightstone appear to float on the surface of the sea. If there is an accompanying onshore wind the waves will be huge, crashing over the sea-wall with spectacular violence. On those days, and it's even better at night, when the sea is really

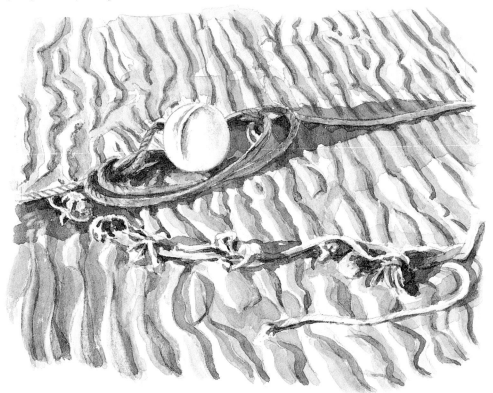

whacking in, there is powerful entertainment to be had. Running the curve of the
promenade, dodging the slap of the sea as it fizzes over the seawall, children set out for
the inevitable delicious soaking as they 'run the prom.' They are even more delighted if
their parents get caught out by a rogue wave. Then everyone joins in, dashing up and
down getting wonderfully wet. In winter it is even more painfully exquisite as the cold
sets in and your teeth rattle in your head. The best places for the High Tide Specials are
north of the Grand Pier - especially the Marine Lake esplanade and the bit of promenade
where it constricts below the Royal Pier Hotel near Anchor Head. All these vary
depending on the direction of the wind and, at times, the danger factor can be real.
I have always felt the town should promote this spectacle, but it is another thing Westonians
seem to keep to themselves! And the pleasure of that hot chocolate afterwards.

[15]*Spring tides have nothing to do with the season. It is the time in the month when the gravitational*
tug of the sun and the moon upon the oceans is in the same line, and therefore at its strongest.
Neap tides occur when the sun and the moon are at right angles to the earth and, to some extent,
cancel one another out. Both sorts of tides occur at fortnightly intervals.

When the tidal fall is at its smallest they are called Neap tides. The sea doesn't come in much - often barely kissing the seawall at Knightstone - but at the same time it stays in longer and doesn't go out as far. So in many ways the sea is more accessible on the neap. There just isn't as much of it. Neap tides are probably better for sailing and generally splashing around and the sea in the bay is, at this time, remarkably shallow. I remember a time when I was test sailing a boat with three friends - we had spent the whole winter sanding and varnishing it. We had already rowed out beyond the Grand Pier before we realised that the boat was filling up with water. We had forgotten to put in the drain plug! Alarm. Panic! Wailing for mother. Loss of all hands. Fevered rowing to little avail. I decided to swim for the shore and on abandoning ship found myself standing in just 18 inches of water looking down on my desperate 'sinking' companions.

I was also standing in warm mud. It was very comforting. In Weston the mud cannot be ignored. The town gets lumbered with name calling such as Weston-super-Mud and from its very beginnings has struggled to deal with the Mystery of the Missing Sea. For all the brickbats, this viscous ooze has a lot going

for it. It brings a glittering violet light to the bay. As the sea retreats, the mud acquires a metallic quality like mercury. It shimmers and at the point where the sea ends and the mud begins the waves appear to solidify. The quality of the light in Weston is often extraordinary. In attempting to capture it, a painting can appear unreal with the purple grey blues of the sea zone, a cobalt green sky and a lowering winter sun.

The mud does have a few disadvantages. It can suck your boots off. It can lurk an inch or two under the sand and then slip like chocolate over your shoes. It is not a good plan to try and walk across the mud region of the bay because you can end up getting stuck and exhausted. The tide may decide to come in - and it can come in at high speed. At the Uphill end of the beach (where parking is allowed) cars that have been driven out that bit too far, can sink and get stuck up to their axles. Their owners then have to watch despairingly as the sea advances.....

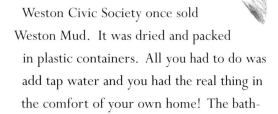

Weston Civic Society once sold Weston Mud. It was dried and packed in plastic containers. All you had to do was add tap water and you had the real thing in the comfort of your own home! The bath-houses on Knightstone also used it in various spa treatments and cures. The warm mud that had so caressed my toes also soothed aching rheumatic joints and painful muscles.

The sandy margin where the beach fades into the mud zone is inhabited by many interesting creatures, but the most evident are the spaghetti worm hills of the lug-worm. Each squiggle of sand has an accompanying dimple, about an inch across, with a small hole in its floor. These mark either end of the lug-worm's U-shaped burrow and are a complete giveaway to the fishermen who dig them up for bait. So it's not unusual to come across even bigger piles of sand which spell out the demise of a number of lug-worms rudely disturbed from their U-bend retreats. Fishing is a popular sport from the beach or from the heights of Knightstone and Birnbeck. On the beach, the middle tides between neap and spring are best for rod and line. In their season these bring in the codfish - themselves trawling for shrimp in the sandy shallows.

Weston Bay has two main areas for boating. Knightstone Harbour is the mooring place for pleasure craft, fishing and motor boats. The wide slipway makes it possible to take a boat trailer right down to the water's edge. It is from here most power craft are launched and water skiers take off. On a good tide and a sunny day Knightstone assumes an animated Mediterranean air. There are boats coming and going. Skiers whizzing back and forth. People peering over railings, gazing down as the Bristol Queen collects a bevy of excited children for a trip around the islands. The second boating place is at the other end of the bay, at Uphill. In the angle of Brean Down and Weston Bay lies the estuary of the River Axe. The Axe is a small, but important river, which may well have been navigable as far as Axbridge a good few centuries ago. It now drains the levels between Bleadon and Brent Knoll - land which is crisscrossed by a network of rhynes and ditches, all of which eventually empty their waters into the Axe. At the estuary mouth, Weston yacht club has its headquarters and, a bit further up stream, is Uphill Boatyard and Marina. Despite the tidal challenge, this is a popular place for dinghies and various sailing craft. With the tidal rise and fall, boats spend a lot of their lives stranded on the river's mud banks, and to get a good sail timing is all important. If you are not careful, you can be stranded out in the bay waiting for the next tide. Another hazard is Black Rock, standing sentry at the estuary mouth. Black Rock's summit always stands clear of the sea and it serves as an important navigational marker - particularly so when Uphill was a small port for coal and similar cargoes. Apparently Black Rock marked the western limit of the Forest of Mendip under the Saxon and Norman kings.

Black Rock, The Axe Estuary

Chapter Four

BREAN DOWN

Although it plays such a large part in the dramatic action of Weston Bay, Brean Down actually belongs to the village of Brean (Bree-un to the locals). The estuary of the River Axe, which could only be crossed by an occasional summer ferry at Uphill, effects a real separation from Weston and ensures the Down's isolation. The small road to Brean from the A370 does the same thing as it wriggles its way across the rhyned levels, often travelling in quite the opposite direction to the one anticipated! All this adds up to a journey of nearly nine miles - a long way for somewhere that appeared to be just outside your front door.

Brean Down from Anchor Head, late afternoon

Brean itself is chockful with caravans, but the walk up to and along the crest of the Down is full of expectation and reward; a cadence to the Mendip Hills and Crooks Peak[16] climbing away to the east. Brent Knoll hill is in the near-ground and Glastonbury Tor, misty Avalon, far off in the distant south-east. There is the sweep of the Bristol Channel, the islands and to the north Weston Bay.

[16] *Crooks Peak or Crook Peak? It is a debate that has been going on for a few hundred years !*
It's always been Crooks Peak to me.

The Brean Down headland is the longest of the three promontories (the others being Worlebury and Sand Point) which are such a feature of this part of the Somerset coastline. On the Weston side it reaches out about two miles into the sea and its northern slopes, which face the town, are grassed and have areas of bracken and wind-blasted hawthorn. It was on this side that in 1867 an attempt to build a harbour was made. Ominously, the day after the foundation stone was laid, both the stone and its marker buoy were swept away to Steep Holm! In 1872 the partially completed pier was smashed in one of Weston's Great Storms and the Brean Down Harbour Company collapsed with losses of £ 350,000 - an enormous amount in those days.

On the southern side there are steep cliffs which are a recognised rock climbing challenge. The climbs have enticing names like 'Torpedo' (extremely severe) and 'Cyclops Gatepost' (merely difficult). On these southerly rocks and crags grows the beautiful White Rock Rose - Brean Down is one of the few places where it thrives. You can also find samphire here; a succulent member of the parsley family which used to be collected as a vegetable and for pickling - a risky task which Shakespeare describes in King Lear as "that dreadful trade". (I have also seen samphire growing on the cliffs at Birnbeck)

From the Weston promenade it is possible to make out Brean Down Fort with the naked eye - just visible at the tip of the promontory. When you've walked along the heights of the headland, more than a mile out into the sea, the barracks and gun batteries are an intriguing and climactic conclusion.[17]

[17] Brean Down Fort is one of four forming a defensive chain across the Bristol Channel - the other sites being - Steep Holm - Flat Holm - Lavernock Point in Wales. They were built, at the instigation of Prime Minister Lord Palmerston, in response to the fear of a French invasion in the 1860s. Constructed to a very high standard, they were equipped with the latest rifled muzzle loading (RML) 7 inch guns and mountings. The defences were reinstated during the Second World War.

The fort was badly damaged in 1900 when a soldier - later judged to have been temporarily insane - fired his gun into an ammunition magazine, and blew up himself and part of the fort. What was suspected to be his skull was found some years later by a picnicking party! The fine Victorian masonry of the barracks has survived reasonably intact, and the National Trust, which has owned the Down since 1954, has now acquired the fort itself and is restoring it.

Chapter Five

THE ISLANDS

Gazing out to sea from the Weston promenade, your eyes irresistibly come to rest on the islands Steep Holm and Flat Holm. It is told that a visitor asked which one was which..... From Weston's perspective Steep Holm is shaped like a currant bun, and Flat Holm like a Welsh cake. There are two other islands: Knightstone and Birnbeck, although they no longer quite count in that they are both joined to the mainland by stone or iron causeways. Also, they are not surrounded by water at all states of the tide.

As a boy, staring out to sea through the cloudy promenade telescopes, Steep Holm always seemed a remote and mysterious place. Few people, so far as I could tell, ever got there or knew very much about it. When I did eventually cross that five mile stretch of water in the 1970s and stepped down the gangplank from the Weston Lady onto the shingle beach - it really was a bit like landing on the moon.

Approcahing Steep Holm

Steep Holm rises 78m above the sea. From Weston we can see its small pebbled beach, and the sycamore wood through which a path zigzags to the top. Our view of the island is an illusion - it really isn't shaped like a currant bun at all. We look at its widest end, and it tapers away, like a teardrop, to its western tip known as Rudder Rock. The beach slopes up to a quay constructed during the early part of the Second World War - it was built largely with stone blocks filched from one of the Victorian gun emplacements on the island. As you ascend the cliff path you come to the remains of the island inn - now partly restored - which used to be the scene of much rumbustious behaviour in Victorian times - until spoilsports from the Inland Revenue put a stop to it. For years it was a semi-ruin and the Army nearly finished it off when they blew it up to clear the path in 1941. Steep Holm was an important part of the Palmerston defensive batteries across the Bristol Channel in the 1860s. The island has six sets of gun emplacements positioned at its west and east ends. They are crafted out of beautifully finished Mendip stone quarried on the mainland. Many of the cannons are lying close to their original emplacements having resisted attempts to salvage them. The Second World War batteries and searchlight positions are not faring so well with mouldering concrete, their heavy iron doors quietly rusting to bits.

Wild Peonies on Steep Holm

The most important thing about Steep Holm is its wildlife. In 1976, the island was purchased as a nature reserve, in memory of Kenneth Allsop, a pioneering journalist and environmentalist. It is the home of the famed Wild Peony and other rare plants. It's likely that these were brought to the island by monks, who lived in a small priory high above the pebble beach, for use in herbal remedies. St. Michael's Priory site (12th century) has been meticulously excavated by the Kenneth Allsop Trust, and has a complicated story to tell. If you are lucky, you may meet a grey seal on the shingle spit. There are cormorants on the northern cliffs and a few hundred perfervid gulls.

In relatively good condition are the Victorian barracks which are the headquarters of the Trust on the island. The building sits on the sunny and sheltered southern side, looking out across Bridgwater Bay to the Quantock Hills. It is always that bit warmer than the mainland - so the short boat journey and exploring the island makes for a captivating day out.[18]

Flat Holm from Steep Holm

Flat Holm,[19] although a different shape, has a similar history to Steep Holm. It too had its Viking raiders and itinerant friars, although no established Priory it seems. It was farmed and (like Steep Holm) used for breeding rabbits for meat - a coney island. A fair bit of smuggling went on too - to the consternation of the Custom and Excise who kept it under special watch. Farming was relatively successful here and there were, probably for centuries, farm buildings of some kind on the island. During the 18th century the farmhouse was rebuilt to just about what exists today. It is an ample dwelling with an adjoining walled garden, cottages and sheds. For a while, from 1884, the island was used for cholera isolation and in 1896 a hospital was erected, though hardly ever used. Flat Holm also has Victorian gun emplacements similar to Steep Holm, although the guns were installed in protective pits.

[18] *The Kenneth Allsop Trust runs frequent boat trips to Steep Holm, usually from Knightstone, at weekends and Bank Holidays. The trips run from April to October and are dependent on tide times and the weather. There is comfortable seating in the barracks building where refreshments are available. The island has its own stamps and other souvenirs. Check it out at the Tourist Information Centre. The full account is told in 'Steep Holm - the Story of a Small Island' by Stan and Joan Rendell, and in a number of books by Rodney Legg.*

[19]*Holm is the Danish word for a river island, a legacy from Viking times, particularly the 10th century when the Holms were used as bases from which to raid the mainland.*

The Lighthouse on Flat Holm

For all that, what really distinguishes Flat Holm[20] is its lighthouse. In the early 1700s several attempts to establish a light were refused until 1736 when a ship was wrecked near the Holmes with the loss of 60 soldiers. This tragedy spurred fresh action and in 1737 a tower was built topped by a coal fired brazier. Close by Flat Holm, to the north west, are some deadly rocks known as the Wolves. It was here that in 1817 another boat sank and this time 40 people drowned. This stimulated alterations to the stone tower and by 1820 a new fixed white light was installed. Since then advancing technology has improved the light output - nowadays the light has a flashing pattern of white and red three times every ten seconds. In May 1988 the three lighthouse keepers left the island and the light became fully automatic.

On foggy nights the light would be of little use and then a powerful fog-horn would be sounded. On such nights I remember being tucked up in bed on Worlebury and listening to the visceral, stentorian blasts - they sounded like a forsaken leviathan, far out at sea. It was a dangerous noise, and I would pull the blankets a bit further over my head.

[20]*Flat Holm is not readily accessible from Weston. The island lease is held by South Glamorgan County Council and visits are best arranged from the Welsh side.*

Chapter Six

THE TOWN - PART 1

Walking eastwards
down Regent Street,
away from the Grand
Pier, the first proper
road you come to is
St. James Street on your
right. This used to be
home to Fish and Chip
shops like Farr's, Coffin's
and the Continental.
These have now given way
to restaurants specialising in
Italian, Greek and Asian
food. Weston still has plenty
of fish and chip shops -

*Art Deco
Elephant head,
The Burtons Building*

on the sea-front and in the town proper.
Coffin's have moved to a neo-Victorian restaurant on Alexandra Parade.
From its southern end, St. James Street looks across to Dolphin Square,[21]
a 1960s shopping precinct. This clashes with the 19th century character of the street,
which is still there, just about, at the first floor level and above. In many ways,
St. James Street is a lost opportunity - even ten years ago it was still a charming mix
of cottage shops and Edwardian frontages.

---

[21]*Dolphin Square was a controversial development in the late 1960s and came about with the destruction
of a residential community centred around Carlton Street. An attractive small square and streets were lost
despite much local anguish. Dolphin Square's hard geometry has been softened with the installation of large
protective umbrellas. It is the home of ten-pin bowling.*

Regent Street itself houses the rear extension of Marks and Spencer. Accompanying it, on the north side, is the Burton's building, with its jazzy Art Deco facade of elephants, wrapping itself around into the High Street. On the opposite side of the road Barclays Bank occupies an old Wesleyan Chapel. The intersection of Regent Street and the High Street defines two separate eras. To the south, the buildings are largely post-war and have an uncompromising severity. To the north, it is quite different as the High Street describes a gentle oscillation, following the line of the original village street. The shops, mostly three storey, are an attractive shuffled pack of early and late Victoriana, Art Deco, a former chapel (Woolworth's) and a few post-war insertions. This part of the High Street is a car free zone. Mid-way is the main entrance to the Sovereign Centre, a covered shopping mall with a high glazed atrium at its heart. Its scale fits in comfortably with the rest of the High Street and it is a successful mixture of shops, restaurants, see-through lifts and 900 car-parking spaces! It also provides an imaginative electric scooter scheme for the disabled and a covered way through to Victoria Square and the promenade. The animated clock is a great attraction for children young and old.

Cecil Walker's shop front

HUMILITY

The Sovereign Centre's atrium runs through to its north entrance behind the Italian Gardens[22] at the end of the main High Street. The whole of this area forms a town square and the present division between the two planted zones makes little sense. The formal stone seating and statuary could be repositioned in a lowered central area which would be more sheltered. This would also make it more comfortable for the Farmers' Market which is endeavouring to become established here. Even as they are, the Italian Gardens have a pleasing formality, where shops and shoppers take a breather, the sea just over the shoulders of the Winter Gardens.

[22] *This part of Weston was badly damaged during the last war - especially that part of the High Street facing the Italian Gardens. You will see that this is mainly 1960s rebuilding. The town never quite got over the loss of Lance & Lance, a John Lewis department store, which occupied all of the Waterloo Street / High Street corner site. Walker and Ling, together with Cecil Walker's, are two of the last local firms to remain in the High Street. Cecil Walker's attractive shop was part of the entrance to the Royal Arcade which used to run through to Regent Street. The arcade was largely lost to incendiary bombs. What survived later made way for the Sovereign Centre.*

The High Street now intersects with South Parade (west) and Waterloo Street (east) - the latter running through to the Boulevard, the town's principal thoroughfare. South Parade at first and second storey level betrays its early 19th century town-house origins (still largely intact) and ends opposite The Royal Hotel[23] with a wonderful Italianate Bath stone building which, up until recently, was the National Westminster Bank. Next to it is The Imperial, formerly The Bath Hotel, whose balcony was once used by the returning officer to declare the results of elections.

Standing on the pavement opposite The Royal Hotel, you are immediately aware of Weston College.[24] Its bulk is quite out of scale with this part of the Victorian town. The late 1990s extension is a considerable improvement and has returned the building to the street. Repainting and new windows have also eased the overwhelming concrete brutalism of the original structure.

The High Street, north of the Waterloo Street junction, feels constricted after the open spaces of the Italian Gardens and its four storey buildings proceed all the way to Grove Park. It contains two of the town's oldest pubs - The London and The Britannia. The London[25] was the scene of the sad murder of Ann Fisher by her husband Joel in 1844. Joel was later publicly hanged in Taunton.

[23] *This is the 'large and profitless inn' described in the introductory history. It opened and closed a number of times between 1805 and 1815. So uncertain were its finances, that when beer was delivered from Worle, a bell was rung to announce its arrival! It was enlarged and its companion Royal Terrace (now the Cabot and Grosvenor Hotels) built in the 1840s. They are fine buildings with classical details - curved windows, verandas and balconies - set in their own tennis lawns stretching down to the sea-front.*

[24] *In the mid-1960s Somerset County Council pushed through the design in the face of considerable local opposition. It was supposed to provide 'a really vigorous piece of punctuation'. Good grief.*

[25] *See Brian Austin's full account in his Tales of Old Weston Volume 2.*

'The Brit'
High Street North

The London is much altered since Joel Fisher's time, but the Britannia, with its own alley way and courtyard, is tucked away from the hurly-burly of the street, and has managed to hold on to its 19th century character. The high buildings which proceed from the Britannia have elaborately worked Bath stone facades designed by Hans Price. Interposed is the 1960s frontage of the Playhouse - the original, which was destroyed by fire in 1964, was set back from the road forming a small covered square, busy with stalls and small shops. Opposite the Britannia, West Street runs seawards to meet the stable block of the Royal Hotel. In village Weston this was West Lane and, although war damage has meant some rebuilding, it has managed to retain its intimacy. Shops along its south pavement are especially attractive - carved animal heads above a former butcher's, and a trio of arches forming the windows of another. Excellent bread is to be found at Astill's Bakery [26] on the north side.

[26] *Up until the 1980s, Weston had many small, family run bakeries making beautiful yeasty bread. Passmore's at Bournville, Durston's of Milton Road, Nan's in Orchard Street... At the time of writing only the Whitecross Bakery and Astill's survive.*

St. John's Church and the Glebe House

Wadham Street, which runs north from West Street to Grove Park, has also managed to hold on to its early buildings. Weston Civic Society has been busy here restoring the large red brick Victorian stables and workshops along the east side. This is now the Society's headquarters; the Heritage Centre, which comes complete with restaurant and exhibitions. Further up the street the society's offspring building trust has been responsible for the adaption of a Baptist Church (early Hans Price) into The Blakehay,[27] an Arts and Community Centre, which now has a raked auditorium and adjoining meeting and exhibition rooms.

[27]*Blakehay was the name given to an area of land between where Wadham Street now lies and Grove Park. Blake = black and Hay = fenced field - a fenced area of dark soil.*
See Weston-super-Mare. A History and Guide. Philip Beisly.

The Heritage Centre

In the early 1980s Weston-super-Mare Civic Society bought a large, dilapidated, late Victorian, red-brick building in Wadham Street. It had started life as a coach house and wine store, and during the Second World War served as a base for the Air Raid Patrol. It then became a book repair factory, and during the 1960s, a Jazz club (the 'JL'), which later turned

to Rock and Roll. Through various community schemes, managed by the Civic Society, it has been converted into a combination of exhibition areas, a coffee house/restaurant, offices and a home for the Society. The main exhibition tells the story of Weston; from the fishermen's cottages to the present day. There is an intriguing bird's eye view of the original village, with the story moving through the dramatic growth of the Victorian town, and how the houses were designed and built. A wall, outside the exhibition room, is filled with a huge scale Ordnance Survey map of the town in 1880. It even gives the original house names and garden designs! The exhibition ends with a mad, mechanical, beach scene - overlooked, with some disapproval, by a yellow eyed gull. The restaurant has a vegetarian bias and does a brisk lunchtime trade. At other times it is the perfect place to relax with a pot of Darjeeling and a toasted teacake.

Across the street is the Blakehay, a Hans Price Baptist Church, rescued by the Society's offspring building trust. It now serves as a small concert hall (250 seats), with adjoining exhibition rooms and community centre.

Lovers' Lane links Grove Park to Lower Church Road where Hans Price's masterpiece, the School of Science and Art, faces us. Price's use of glazed and terracotta panels, high studio windows and carved stone is typical of the Arts and Craft movement of late Victorian England. Despite being such a strong building, it is almost subsumed by its towering offspring Weston College.

Stone Lintel, South Terrace

To the north of Lovers' Lane, on a bluff above the tennis courts, stands the parish church of St. John the Baptist and just below to the east, its former rectory the Glebe House.[28] In 1824, the 13th century church was considered too small and mean to satisfy Weston's burgeoning population, so it was pulled down and replaced by the present building. A case of ecclesiastical vandalism? So the town lost an important part of its mediaeval past and bits of the old church were carried off and incorporated in secular buildings around the town - some getting as far as gateposts in Worle! Directly opposite St. John's is the stately Bath stone facade of Oriel Terrace. It has a lightness of touch about it which complements the church perfectly and it's good to see some of the gate pillars and railings being restored. Across the road from Lovers' Lane runs South Terrace which meets up with the Royal Crescent and Park Place - already described in Chapter 1. Along the seaward side, South Terrace has some very early seaside residences (called Park Villas and which front onto Victoria Walk) and then - lo and behold! - some of the windows at no.7 (Oriel Lodge) have carved stone lintels recycled from the old church!

Standing at the southern end of Royal Crescent, looking across the former parkland of Park Place, you long for the judicious landscaping which would restore the setting of some of the town's best buildings.

[28] *The Glebe House dates back to, at least, the mid-17th century, although it has been much altered over the years. It is known that Rector Christopher Sadbury, a royalist, locked up unruly villagers in the house during the Civil War. In 1790, a hundred years after the Pigott family from Brockley acquired the Manor, a younger son, Rev. Wadham Pigott, was curate at the parish church. It was he who probably set in train the improvements to Grove Cottage and the Glebe House to accommodate his artistic friends.*

Chapter Seven

THE TOWN - PART 2

*The Weston and Somerset
Mercury building*

The corner where High Street and Waterloo Street meet must be Weston's windiest place. You either battle against prevailing westerlies to get into High Street - or leave it blown inside out, along with your umbrella. The broad pavement on the south side of Waterloo Street was part of an early road widening scheme which, mercifully, never came about. All this area was occupied by the long lamented Lance & Lance department store, bombed in 1942. One shop here - Leaver's - has been a family-run hardware and ironmongers since the late nineteenth century. The original shop was in High Street (no. 36). The street, from Leaver's to the Weston Mercury office,[29] returns to the original building line whereupon it opens out into the Boulevard. The south side buildings are three and four storeys with pleasing brick and Bath stone details - there's even space for a statue - and they conclude with Hans Price's extraordinary medieval confection; the Weston Mercury offices. Who says the Victorians didn't have a sense of humour! The Mercury's balconied tower is now only palely echoed on the opposite side of the road by the Constitutional Club's truncated castle. This was originally topped by an extraordinary half-timbered turret. The turret was forfeited by neglect in 1981. So the Boulevard lost its Grand (and delightfully crazy) Entrance.

In spite of that, the Boulevard is dramatically different from other streets in the town. It was here that John Wadham Smyth-Pigott, Lord of the Manor, had a special plan. He loved Paris and it was on his insistence that this road reflected the wide and straight avenues of France. It was aligned on the spire of Christ Church, making a splendid finale to the gabled prospect of the tree lined street.[30] It remains a fine road with generous pavements, ideal for street cafes, even though the view of Christ Church has been marred by the intrusion of 1960s semi-detached houses.

[29] *The Weston Mercury, the town's newspaper, remained in local family control until the 1980s. It started out in 1843 as a monthly news-sheet called The Westonian produced by Mr. James Dare. His hand printing press can be seen at the Weston museum. From 1845 it had a keen rival: the Weston Gazette, printed in Wadham Street. The two papers frequently took up opposing political positions, often alternating from one side to the other! They merged in 1951.*

[30] *The Boulevard was originally planted with a mixture of elms and London planes. In the 1950s the Parks Department took it upon itself to replace them with Japanese cherries. I remember the felling of those trees as I walked to Christ Church School. The Kanzan cherry blossom is a blousy show for a week or two in spring - if the wind cooperates - but the trees are poorly shaped and sickly for the rest of the time. As they die they are being replaced with native 'Double Gean' cherries and small leafed ash trees.*

The Boulevard, Spring time

On the south side of the Boulevard, in its westerly third, is Weston Decorators; another long established local business. It occupies an 1880s building which has ironwork and terracotta detailing on its frontage. The sports shop abutting the Mercury office has an elaborate gable end and its large windows betray its previous use as a photographer's studio. Most buildings in this group have an Arts and Crafts mood about them. They are older cousins to the School of Science and Arts (described previously). They were all designed by Hans Fowler Price whose former office at 28, Waterloo Street was still home to a firm of architects until very recently.

Crossing the Boulevard onto its north side, an extended terrace runs down to the junction with Victoria Quadrant. These have always served as both offices and residential flats. Only no. 23 has managed to keep a walled front garden and provide a hint of what this part of the street was like. But no.1 has taken advantage of the south facing pavement and sheltering trees, to set up as an attractive restaurant/patisserie, with tables and chairs on the street.

Crossing Victoria Quadrant, the next terrace has a Gothic style and was once the Smyth Pigott Estate Office. The crab apple tree in the front garden of no. 25 is a local institution - its fruit has an endearing habit of making cidery pavements in the autumn. The block of flats, Tivoli Mansions,[31] was built in the 1980s and has a peculiar sideways stance to the street. Thankfully its two storey frontage has preserved the Boulevard vista.

Continuing along the north side, to where the Boulevard sidesteps right to become Gerard Road, there is a mixture of large detached and semi-detached stone houses. Most have kept their front walls and some their gardens. Stafford Place is one of the few roads to have held onto its original planting of London Plane trees.

The intersection with Alfred Street and Albert Quadrant marks the concluding easterly third of the Boulevard and on its north-east corner stands a splendid Holm oak. The Alfred Street corner is occupied by the old General Hospital which has been converted, with great sensitivity, into spacious apartments.[32]

[31] *This area was occupied by the Summer and Winter Gardens in Victorian times. It then became home to the Tivoli Cinema which was bombed during the war. The Victoria Bowling Club, which nestles behind the new building, is the sole representative of the old Gardens.*

[32] *The original dispensary/hospital in Alfred Street was built between 1857 and 1865 and gradually enlarged with additional wards. In the 1920s Henry Butt orchestrated public opinion and achieved the construction of the large Boulevard wing. It is beautifully fashioned and on the facings the hard Weston limestone has been worked like courses of brick.*

This conversion was a defining moment in the architectural history of the town. For years Weston Civic Society had insisted this group of buildings was too important to be lost. This was emphasised in 1988 when all the Victorian hillside received Conservation Area status. There was considerable confusion over ownership of the hospital site - the Church of England had retained an interest since its original donation of the land. Eventually delay made it possible for the developers to buy the site economically and to retain and adapt the most important buildings.

Further on from the old hospital (now Henry Butt House) stands another Hans Price contribution - the Public Library (1900). Unusual for Weston in that it is constructed largely of dark red brick with relieving bands of Bath stone. The arched doorway is watched over by Six Muses. The library and reading rooms originally occupied the ground floor with the town's museum upstairs. In 1975, the museum departed for Burlington Street, and the library now inhabits the whole building. The south side of the Boulevard closes with the 1950s telephone exchange - its flat planes of glass and metal have always sat unhappily in the Victorian street.

'The Muses,' Weston Central Library

Around the corner in Alfred Street, set back from the road, is Weston's original hospital and dispensary (1857). Hans Price yet again. This time, early in his career, his design has a simplicity which has been recaptured in the recent redevelopment. Across the road, the adaption of the old depository buildings has not been so successful, although it has preserved the busy roof line of Alfred Street. What used to be Christ Church Hall,[33] on the corner of Prospect Place, now houses a remarkable collection of Lambretta motor scooters. In Burlington Street, the Museum (The Time Machine) occupies the former Gas Company offices. Looking out across their gardens, directly opposite the museum, is a charming group of houses called Meadow Villas. It's a great shame the setting of these attractive buildings is spoilt by a hotch potch of garages, hard-standing and a disguised gas device. At one time this area was a small market garden.

[33] *I used to have school dinners here and difficulty with rice pudding. We would troop in convoy from Christ Church School waving to patients smoking their cigarettes on the hospital balconies. The school dentist also pulled out two of my teeth in a room on the first floor - even though I had a letter saying he mustn't. These things stay with you.*

Alfred Street carries on south, past the Meadow Street/Baker Street intersection, with terraces of two and three storey town houses which open directly onto the pavement. It has lost most of its shops. Meadow Street, like the High Street which it eventually joins, is a remnant of the former village and follows a meandering way. As the village changed into a town, Meadow Lane (as it then was) became occupied by a mixture of workshops, pubs and shops which served the town's working families. It remains a marvellous mixture of businesses and is one of Weston's great assets. It's here that you can get your keys cut, your trousers altered, guitar strings, fresh veg from Kellands, games, Army surplus, your hair dressed, coal-effect fires, coal effect hair...... In 1942, after it was bombed out of High Street, Marks and Spencer took up residence in the shop on the western corner of Meadow Street and Orchard Place.

Running north and south from Meadow Street are residential roads including Alma Street, Hopkins and Palmer Streets.[34]

Each of these has its own character, partly depending on the materials used in their construction, the width of the street and the vista it opens on to. Palmer Street is rather classily finished in local stone whereas other streets, which are a bit older, are mostly rendered. Some of the houses have tiny front gardens and others front doors that open directly onto the street. In Alma Street particularly, houses have been pushed up a social notch or two by the addition of a fine bay window.

Boswell's, Alexandra Parade

Behind many of these houses are workshops and stables, usually revealed by arched passage-ways. Above the archways sit an additional room or two - little space is wasted. Tucked away behind these terraces are forgotten cottages, probably as old as the village. Surrounded by the advancing streets they became lost from view. They remain hidden, forsaken memories with lost lives.

In Cross Street, which runs between Alma Street and Orchard Street, there is a three storey building which was originally a corn chandler's business. It came complete with a high loading door but recently its simple classical proportions have been wrecked by ugly uPVC windows and infilling. There are other back ways, between Meadow Street and Alexandra Parade with hidden entrances and exits, where the backland of an older Weston can still be found.

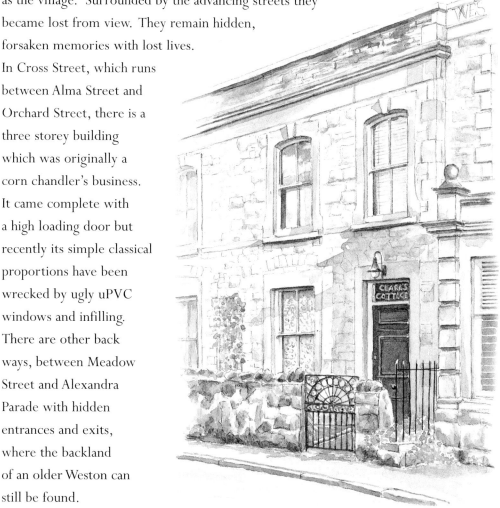

Clara's Cottage, Burlington Street

[34]*It is difficult to believe that the 1960s Town Plan demarcated the Palmer Street area for demolition in order to build a central car park! Planning blight undermined a thriving community and many of the houses were sold to the council at depressed prices and families moved to outlying estates with great sadness. Only when the threat of destruction was lifted did the area return to what it was before - houses in the heart of the town, perfect for older people and for those who neither want or need a car.*

Chapter Eight

THE TOWN - PART 3

To the south, Alfred and Orchard Streets open out into Alexandra Parade. This area has changed enormously over the past 25 years, mainly through the construction of the large Tesco store on old railway land. Indeed, the railway has long had a close connection with this part of the town. It was here the horse-drawn railcarriages on the original branch line came to a halt. Westonians had decided they did not want the steam railway in their genteel midst, so the Bristol and Exeter Railway Company diverted the track to open moorland outside the town! The horses drew up just where the Floral Clock now stands. The pub close by, at the time of writing called 'Jack Stamps,' was originally the Railway Inn. When the railway withdrew to its fine establishment in Station Approach this area was called Old Station Square, and planted out with trees and lawns. It became known as 'The Plantation,' and the name is still used by many who have lived in the town all their lives. Other than the Floral Clock (1935), the only remnant of the old landscaping is the quaint half-timbered weighbridge kiosk stranded on its own islet at the eastern end of the Parade.

Various traffic schemes have succeeded in converting this open space into a race track which you traverse in fear of your life! The planting of Horse chestnut trees (by the Civic Society), around the circumference of the central lawned island, has rescued the original Plantation to some extent, but the high speed traffic flow still needs to be hugely modified.

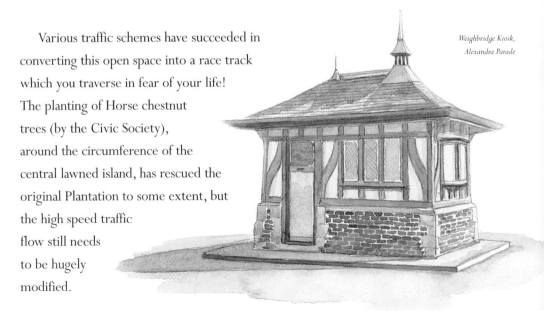

Weighbridge Kiosk, Alexandra Parade

Tesco pushes up against the Odeon Cinema whose flat Deco tower is the dominant feature of the Parade. The Odeon[35] was part of 'The Centre' shopping development in 1935 which originally included a glass canopied pavement curving away towards the Town Hall. Sadly, the Art Deco style has become debased as original windows and shop fronts have been lost. Virtually all of the protective canopy has gone. And so has the last mature lime tree which grew directly opposite the Town Hall entrance, felled while I was writing this.

[35] *The Odeon itself had a major restoration a few years ago with many of its black vitreous tiles being replaced. It remains a fine building. The main theatre has been divided into two, but the screen sizes have not been sacrificed. In addition, two studio theatres have been cleverly fitted in. The ambience of the stairway to a first floor lounge, complete with languorous settees, remains a distinct cinema experience. The luminous Compton Organ is still there, rising and falling, with lights aglow on special occasions.*

Walliscote Road runs north/south from The Odeon for nearly a mile. Magdala Buildings, opposite the cinema, curves around the corner into Alexandra Parade. These shops and offices, designed by Hans Price in 1869, linked the burgeoning High Street with the Town Hall area. Its elegantly fashioned Bath stone facade has worn well, and the neo-Victorian frontage of Coffin's fish restaurant is an excellent example of sympathetic design. A small cobbled back lane divides Magdala Buildings from the 'Town Crier' pub which sits on the corner of Oxford Street opposite the Town Hall. This used to be called the Bristol and Exeter Hotel; a direct link with the company which brought the railway to Weston.

The Town Hall,
the old main entrance

Oxford Street runs east/west from The Centre to the sea-front. Along its northern pavement, lies Southbourne Terrace. Although shops and restaurants have filled up the terrace's front gardens, the original building, can still be seen; peering down from its first and second floors. Except for the Town Crier, nothing remains from the Victorian period at street level. Across the road things are quite different with the Town Hall and Emmanuel Church.

Building the first Town Hall took place amid furious allegations of corruption, but was eventually completed in 1858-59. In 1897 Hans Price succeeded, brilliantly, in absorbing the earlier hall into the present self-assured public building. It came complete with a new clock tower which owes quite a bit to Big Ben, and a gabled meeting room astride a five arched portico. It remains a fine building, despite the ponderous 1980 annex. Part of the earlier Town Hall, which contains the old Borough Council Chamber, can still be seen from Oxford Street; in the small open area next to the churchyard.[36]

Emmanuel Church, Weston's second church, was built in 1847 and came to be through the extraordinary energies of a young curate of the parish church - Rev. John Hamilton Forsyth. He was known for his devotion to the poor - this was very much the working class area of the town - and he died just as building on his church was completed. The church tower has some fearsome gargoyles at its summit, looking out over the town with general disapproval. Not measuring up to John Hamilton Forsyth's expectations I suspect!

[36] When unloved Avon County Council was disbanded in 1996, Woodspring District Council
metamorphosed into the North Somerset Council - the culmination of 20 years
campaigning for the town to 'Return to Somerset.'
In order to accommodate the enlarged authority, the Assembly Room of the 1858
Town Hall was sympathetically furnished as the Council Chamber.
The fitting out, using cherry wood and other natural
materials, has succeeded in rejuvenating what was a lacklustre and underused hall.
With the refurbishment, beautiful encaustic floor tiles were revealed
in the entrance lobbies and the meeting room, above the entrance portico,
returned to its Hans Price proportions.

South of the Town Hall is Hans Price's finest Weston building, for me anyway - Walliscote School. This was formerly known as the Board School. It is made up of a series of high roofed pavilions[37] linked by single floored gabled rooms. The roof peaks are crowned with elaborate ventilation 'lanterns' and the theme of high and low roofs is repeated in smaller buildings to the rear. There is also an intriguing, timbered, Arts and Crafts out-building, tucked mysteriously round the back. The whole formation of roofs and ventilators catches the sun - Bath stone and high lanterns glow with reflected light. It is an education - just in itself.

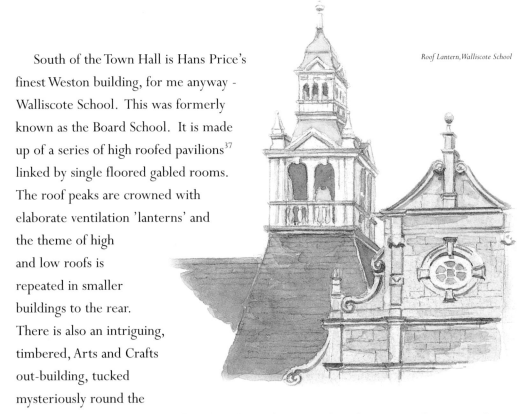

Roof Lantern, Walliscote School

From the Town Hall, Station Road runs eastwards to the Railway Station with Tesco's store to the north. On its southern side stand the Court House and Victoria Methodist Church which impart a rather serious air to the street. Nightingale's depository building, with high arched loading doorways and small tiled turret, provides a bit of relieving self-confidence. Tesco's occupies what was originally railway land; where Weston's second station was built in 1866. It was here that visitors began to arrive in great numbers - but this was still only a branch line. By 1884 the Great Western Railway Company had completed a new loop line, and that meant the town, at long last, had main line services - something the good citizens had resisted 20 years previously.

[37] *Hans Price's pavilion theme is repeated at Wyvern School (also a former Board/Council School and later called Winterstoke Secondary School for Girls/Ashcombe Primary) in Locking Road, which has recently been saved from extinction by conversion into flats. The work has been carried out by Fisher and Dean; the same firm who rescued the former General Hospital in the Boulevard.*

The new station, Weston's third, was built bestriding the new line with high chimneys and using local stone. The Victorian station is largely intact, mostly single storeyed and embracing both sides of the track, although some of its Great Western character was lost when the glazed canopies were replaced with modern approximations. The embossed cast-iron columns and fret-work detailing remain while trains still arrive and depart along platforms where the lines follow a satisfying curve. It's easy to imagine coal fires burning in the waiting-rooms, and the blast of steam locomotives preparing to depart. Across the road from the station is an engaging group of 1930s flat roofed houses. They still look challengingly modern and must have appeared revolutionary in their day. It's a shame that the horizontal iron frame windows have largely lost out to the ubiquitous uPVC.

Waiting for the train, late afternoon

GOUGH HOUSE

Moving on south from the Town Hall and past Walliscote School, we enter an area of the town where grand houses generally preside. Some have towers and turrets, with bay windows that provide a panoramic view of the street. The large windows allowed more light into rooms which the Victorians perversely cancelled out with heavy curtains, to protect their furnishings from the sun! At least the sombre colours gave the servants an easier time by disguising the coal dust. Wilton Gardens, a small square, chopped off by Walliscote Road, has rather smaller detached and semi-detached villas (with names like Pembroke and Woodville) arranged around a walled garden. Along its north side there is a yellow brick terrace which would be more at home in Notting Hill, W11. A curious translocation. Just beyond Wilton Gardens is a house called 'Varzin,' at 42, Walliscote Road. It is the boyhood home of Arthur Stanley Eddington (1882-1944), one of the fathers of modern astrophysics. There is a detailed bronze plaque set on the house wall above the pavement, with a relief portrait of the physicist.

Although Ellenborough Park was designed to set off its fine crescent (described in Chapter 2), it also provided a perfect setting for some serious gentlemen's residences. Where Walliscote Road divides the park, on its northern boundary (Ellenborough Park North) are two such dwellinghouses. To the west is Tower House (now called Gough House) with its high garret. From here the retired gentlefolk could watch the setting sun, or the loiterings in the park below. On the eastern corner, set back behind high railings and complete with its coach-house and outbuildings, sits Ellenborough Hall. The coach-house is unusual for Weston where few of the large houses had their own stables. After all, their owners were only middle class, and might even have earned a living from trade!

Hans Fowler Price - Weston's Architect

'Bourn' 7, Trewartha Park

As described in the main text, Hans Fowler Price was responsible for most of Weston's finest architecture. What isn't generally realised is that a huge number of the town's domestic buildings also had their genesis on the drawing boards of his office in Waterloo Street.

Hans Price was born in 1835 at Langford in Somerset. He trained as an architect in Liverpool, and subsequently opened his first office in Weston High Street in 1860. He cannily married Jane Baker, whose brother Samuel was a partner in the Smyth Pigotts' firm of solicitors, and Price eventually became the consulting architect for the Smyth Pigott Estate. He revealed a flare for detail that would make a straightforward house a bit special, and this individuality was maintained when the opportunity arose for his Grand Works. These he carried off with enormous self-confidence, and his buildings are now an inimitable part of the Weston scene. He recruited styles from wherever he fancied. The Mercury Office was apparently inspired by the Cathedral of Saragossa in Spain, the Arts and Crafts movement imbued the personality of the School of Science and Art, medieval Tudor at the Constitutional Club, and a Germanic influence in the draped facades of Walliscote School.

Price and Jane lived at 'Tyn-y-Coed', 48, Hill Road for 30 years, then at 'Bourn' (named after Jane's family home in Burrington), 59, Boulevard. They finally moved to another 'Bourn' at 7, Trewartha Park. They had four daughters and one son. Hans Price was a churchwarden at Christ Church (whose enlargement he designed) and Chairman of the Weston-super-Mare Gas Company. He was also a keen chess player and invited a number of chess champions to play in Weston. The Mercury obituary paints a picture of a man with tremendous energy, who remained mentally active to the last. He was still busy in his office a short while before his death in 1912, aged 77 years. His wife and son had died before him.

South of Ellenborough Park, Walliscote Road intersects with what has been described as 'Villadom.' Most of the houses in Clifton, Clevedon and Severn Roads are late Victorian and they had a dual purpose. They were not just family homes - they also had an extra room or two for paying guest. They are substantial houses, mostly semi-detached, two storey, with bay windows onto the street. They have small front and rear gardens, and a narrow path and wall divides them from the property next door. Although they rarely diverge from the standard villa formula, the hard, light-grey limestone gives them a strong local identity. The houses crowd all sides of the streets with the sea sparkling temptingly in the west.

Originally there were shops on every street corner with one or two tucked in along the street - a few of these still remain in Clevedon and Clifton Roads. Whitecross Road is an old-style shopping area with a baker, newsagents, butcher, greengrocer, a sexual emporium.... The houses, which became shops, sacrificed their front gardens to form the wide pavement which extends down to Severn Road. For many years the shop on the south-east Clevedon Road/Whitecross Road corner, gave its name to this junction - Brown's Corner. The name of the shop, which closed down during WW2, can still be seen in the doorway mosaic. More recently it became Southside Video and is now the Whitecross Community Centre.

Villas, Walliscote Road, looking towards Clarence Park

Chapter Nine

THE HILLSIDE

When, in 1835, the Misses Pank sent their architect from Italy to design a good house in the Italian style, he chose a perfect spot. Halfway up the southern Worlebury hillside, above and west of the parish church, he built a beautiful Italian mansion with windowed towers, stables and servants' quarters, an ice house and a footbridge linking two parts of the main garden. All the buildings were constructed from the softer pink local limestone, and so the house was called The Villa Rosa. It's uncertain how long the Misses Pank were in residence - or if they ever arrived - for, by 1847, the formidable Sophia Rooke had arrived.

The Villa Rosa footbridge, Shrubbery Road

After the Villa Rosa, large houses sprang up along the hill. They were set back in high terraced gardens and built with stone quarried from where the houses were going to stand. The hillside became the most favoured area. It was warm and sheltered. Set magisterially above the town, it enjoyed the panoramic sweep of the bay, and all the sunshine that was going during an English summer.

Villa Rosetta

'Lady' Rooke promoted the development of her Shrubbery Estate and, following her example, similar exclusive enclaves arose on other parts of the hill. They were given high sounding names like Montpelier, Landemann Circus or Eastfield Park and these prestigious groups of houses were usually organised around a large garden or a church. Some exacted a toll for the use of their private roads which were sentried by gatehouses - especially so in 'The Shrubbery.' Sophia sank a well and built a castellated water-tower which supplied the estate. The tower still stands in Shrubbery Avenue and is built with that distinctive Villa Rosa stone. Crossing the small park that the water tower overlooks, you arrive at the top of Shrubbery Road where the road dips steeply between high stone walls with glimpses of the sea beyond. The ballustraded arch of the Villa Rosa Bridge spans the road just here, but the Italian Mansion is missing. The demolition of the Villa Rosa was an act of appalling vandalism and duplicity. Its loss symbolises the crass exploitative developments that struck Weston in the 1970s. The high rise blocks which have appropriated its name are an unfortunate legacy, but a remnant of the old place does still survive. Peeking out over the fence, at the back of the 20th century apartments, is the octagonal tower of the Villa Rosetta. The tower belongs to what was the coach house and stables of the Villa Rosa and, with the footbridge, they all carry the signature pink limestone of the lost house. The stone bridge linked two parts of the garden estate and Sophia Rooke's domain is remembered in the name Rosemary given to the attractive 1920s bungalow built in the eastern garden.

Sophia Rooke's Water Tower

The high Atlantic Terraces, which flank Holy Trinity Church in Atlantic Road, were built in the 1850s and are testament to the enormous self-confidence of the growing town. Five storeys high from basement to attic, their south facing drawing-rooms command quite breathtaking views across Weston and Bridgwater Bays. The very place to spend the summer, far away from the heat and grime of the infernal cities! Atlantic Road is already wide, but is made to feel even more spacious by the fall of the land and long front gardens. The likes of St. Neots and Church Mansions started their lives as large semi-detached houses set in extensive gardens below the high steeple of Holy Trinity. In the 1920s they were converted into mansion flats, and these conversions have often been carried out with great ingenuity using matching stone and windows. It is an intriguing puzzle to sort out just where the changes have taken place - where the original house begins and ends.[38]

[38] *The mansion flat conversions were another of Henry Butt's accomplishments. The wealthy quarry owner saw that the maintenance of large houses was beyond the means of a middle class which had lost its servants. That same middle class still aspired to gentility however, so most of the apartments were contrived to hold on to at least one spacious room.*

Weston Museum - 'The Time Machine'

In 1975, the local council converted the former Weston Gas Company buildings, in Burlington
Street, into a brand new museum, providing a vast increase in space for displays and storage
(prior to that, the museum had squeezed itself into the upper floors of the library building in
the Boulevard). The outstanding feature of the conversion is the central glass-roofed courtyard
with original wood cobbles. The entrance leads through the Museum shop into the courtyard,
from which the display areas are reached on different levels. These galleries exhibit the geology,
archaeolgy and wildlife of the district. The courtyard has marvellous old enamel signs,
an Edwardian chemist shop and seaside tales. You will find some of Laurie Lee's automata here -
as described in his 'Cider with Rosie' and even more spooky than when they resided on the
Grand Pier. Since 1975 the Museum has acquired two adjoining terrace cottages and a hall -
the latter previously belonged to the Plymouth Brethren. One of the small houses -
Clara's Cottage - has been furnished to present a house from the late 1800s. It provides an
intriguing insight into our recent past.

Atlantic Road South has a more
suburban feel. The houses
have held on to their
conservatories and their
gardens and, although
overlooked, refuse to be
overpowered by the high
rise apartments built on
the old tennis courts behind
them. There are even a
couple of early bungalows
(with curious names like
Baveno) tucked in at the
eastern end.

Looking towards Sand Point,
from Prince Consort Gardens

Prince Consort Gardens, a terraced park at the western tip of Worlebury Hill, looks out to sea above Birnbeck Pier. This is truly one of Weston's special places. The whole sweep of the Severn Sea is laid out, from the Quantock Hills and Exmoor in the south, then across the estuary to Barry, Penarth and Cardiff (from where you can see the Millennium Stadium), across the Severn Mouth with the two Severn Bridges, and back home to Sand Point. There's quite a bit in between too; Brean Down, the islands Steep Holm and Flat Holm and, immediately below, the splayed out elegance of Birnbeck Pier and the bright red doors of the Lifeboat House.[39] The graceful slate roofed villas, which overlook Prince Consort Gardens, belong in the main to Weston College - up until 1963 they were the home of Westcliff, a private boarding school for girls.

[39] *The Life boat house was built in 1902 and remains in regular use.*

The gardens are simply laid out with lawns and flowers. The small circular pond appears to have lost its fountain but the secret boating pool is still there, hiding behind the rockery. On a lower terrace, overlooking Birnbeck, is a fine shelter from where the estuary always puts on a great show; gigantic container ships that can dwarf the islands; the changing textures of the ebb and rising tides, and the racing water under the pier causeway. Sometimes the air has a clarity that makes Wales seem an arm's length away, the Holms picked out in sunlight. At others, the Channel is cloaked and mysterious. The pier slides behind a veil, its causeway vanishes into the imagination. On a summer's evening the whole place can become incandescent as the setting sun slides into Wales and the sky becomes a furnace.[40]

Shelter with fine views

[40]*During the year, the setting sun travels a fair distance along the horizon. In high summer it sets behind the Brecon Beacons in the north-west, whereas in winter the day's journey ends at Brean Down. After the winter solstice it starts heading north once again.*

South Road undulates gently along the side of the hill. Big houses with sinuous driveways, fronted by pines and evergreen oak, stand remote and aloof from the road. For part of the way, the southern view of the town has been obscured by selfish fencing,[41] but you are still able to gaze over the chimneyed roofscape of Grove Park Road and beyond.

At its eastern end, South Road takes an S-bend and comes to a halt at the top of Queens Road, at the entrance to the Town Quarry.[42] It then continues its way along the side of the hill as Cecil Road. The quarry is leased from North Somerset Council by Weston Civic Society which has converted it into a small nature reserve and artists' workshops. There is also a recycling scheme in progress. This is a warm and sheltered place which catches the sun, especially in winter. Peregrine falcons nest in the high cliffs where Holm oak and valerian cling on for dear life. Down below, speckled wood and gatekeeper butterflies bounce around the edges of the thickets where the wrens clatter. There is usually a bunch of crows lugging about the cliff tops, behaving abominably. The stone town of Weston came from here. The rock is an extravagant palette of colours - red and yellow ochres, muddy conglomerates and light greys. The pink limestone of the Villa Rosa is here. The town really is blessed with all its beautiful stone, and it should be treasured.

[41] This part of South Road used to look down on the buildings and playing fields of St. Peter's School which was attended by author Roald Dahl and actor/satirist John Cleese. Dahl vividly describes his pre-war school days (not entirely jolly) in his autobiography 'Boy.' In the days of Empire many of the grand houses had become private schools to educate the children of civil servants and managers who lived in 'The Colonies'. St. Peter's was one, others were La Retraite in South Road, Eastern House in Landemann Circus and Hazelhurst Collegiate School for Girls at Glentworth Hall. At one time there were more than thirty such schools in the town. Most faded away after the Second World War.

[42] The quarry was a bit too close to genteel Weston for its comfort. During Victorian times the residents complained bitterly about the noise and the dust but, because the quarry was there first, it all fell on deafened ears. Even lumps of stone arriving on the morning breakfast table was not a strong enough objection! I well remember the explosive thumps when I lived in Queens Road after the war, but no rock ever landed in my puffed wheat.

Redundant buildings sit low down in the excavated quarry bottom from where the escarpment towers above you. This is where the limestone was smashed and pulverised for, towards the end, most of the extracted stone was used for making roads. It's so peaceful now, hard to imagine the dirt and the danger then.

The Old Town Quarry

The Stone Town

During most of the 19th and the earlier part of the 20th centuries, Weston was built
from stone quarried out of Worlebury or Uphill. Weston stone is predominantly
Carboniferous Limestone; a dense, heavy rock, locally light-grey in colour.
There is also a softer, pink limestone - as was used in the Villa Rosa -
which is seen less frequently. The hardness of the grey stone made it difficult to work,
and masons needed great skill and strength to fashion it.
Despite this, house facades often have this stone worked into squared blocks
(dressed stone) giving the building a neat, fashioned appearance.
A softer, Oolitic Limestone from Bath was imported to finish the corners of houses
(quoins), and around the windows. Bath stone is so 'soft' it can be cut with a handsaw.
It is often carved to provide elaborate decoration around windows and doors.
Its softness does make it vulnerable to weathering, and repairs should be with new stone,
or the correct stone mixes. It should never be painted. Other than repointing,
the Carboniferous Limestone never needs repair. It is so durable that the mason's
chisel marks can still be seen after 150 years, and the worked surfaces
remain sharp and defined.

A town built out of its own stone is a unique thing, and it surely won't happen again.
It should be jealously guarded, and that protection needs to include chimney stacks,
garden walls, gate pillars, the wooden sash windows and terracotta roof tiles -
they all give definition to the building and the street. Although many of Weston's
older houses follow pattern book Victorian designs, the high quality of their construction
and the wonderful limestone makes them extraordinary.

Queens Road used to be called Quarry Road (not a 'nice' address) and it leads
down from the quarry to the top of Grove Park. Close by is All Saints Church (1901,
architect George Bodley) which, despite never getting its tower, is recognised as a
fine example of '14th Century Gothic Revival.' Inside it has a spacious and light
atmosphere, and the boarded waggon roof has endowed it with resonant acoustics.
Somehow it's a very modern church. Many of the big houses on this area of the hill have
had the mansion conversion treatment, and have been fused into elaborate terraces.
The cascading terrace in All Saints Road, below the church, is different.
It was designed that way and is unique in Weston.
The houses step down the steep hill with
easy symmetry. Shame on the two
that have sacrificed their gardens
and their front walls.

From a back garden in Stafford Place

Bristol Road Lower (or Lower Bristol Road!) runs from the bottom of Grove Park to the top of Ashcombe Park. A distance of about a mile. Running from it, roads like Southside, Landemann Circus, Eastfield Park and Montpelier all aspired to the grand house tradition of South Road. In Lower Bristol Road itself, the houses have a more domestic scale and, because of that, many have resisted conversion into flats.

Montpelier rises, steeply, up from the town, past the spire of Christ Church (1855). Opposite the church, Christ Church Path runs back down the hill, and continues towards Christ Church School (which Lord Jeffrey Archer and the author attended). Further up, Montpelier Path steps down into Stafford Place and provides an unobstructed view of this part of the hillside. There is still a large tract of sloping land, coombe-like, running up the west side of Montpelier, through the water reservoir and across the road to Eastfield Park. From the back gardens of Stafford Place, with walnut trees and Monterey cypresses, Christ Church steeple (complete with gold weather-cock), the high gables of St. Owens (now Kairos) and Chelford Lodge; you have a perfect village setting. In summer the sky is full of swifts.

The Victorian hillside effectively ends at Ashcombe Cemetery. There are some large houses which back onto the woods along Lower Bristol Road, and up to Manor Road there is a mixture of 1920 and 1930s developments built on the land of Manor Farm. Up to 1970 Manor Road marked the western boundary of the Lodge Estate and, until that time, cows grazed on the slopes below Bristol Road (Lower).

Opposite the farm land, The Lodge[43] itself was hidden behind a tree filled estate which merged into the woods. As with so much else in those doomy days, the old house was demolished and, like the Villa Rosa, only its stables, the coach-house and a few of the trees survive.

[43]*The Lodge was built for the 8th Earl of Cavan in 1863. In the late 1800s it was purchased by John Jeremiah Jackson-Barstow and he lived there with his wife, son and six daughters. He died in 1940 aged 96. His son was killed in the First World War, only one of the daughters married and none had children. The whole family was extraordinary in its devotion to public service. The last daughter, Enid, died in 2000. At that time she lived at the Old Rectory in Christon to where the surviving sisters had moved when the Lodge was sold in the early 1970s.*

The Mediterranean Walls of Weston

Limestone and forgiving lime mortar make the town's older stone walls a fascinating repository of plant life, and it is intriguing how the sunny spots have been colonised by a variety of Mediterranean migrants. In summer, the walls are an astonishing display of purple and blue flowers consisting of two separate species of Campanula - both with impossible names. The more common is Campanula portenschlagiana, the Dalmatian bellflower, which has bright purple bells. Less frequently seen, but just as vigorous, is Campanula poscharskyana which comes from the mountains of Croatia, and has stars of pale lavender-blue. The Dalmatian bellflower is very free flowering and can often be found, still busily in bloom, in dark December. Another southern invader is the Red valerian (Centranthus ruber) whose powerful roots can push walls apart. In the Weston area, it seems to be mostly pink rather than red - although a bank of plants can go through a colour range from white to vermillion. The flower-heads are clusters of small flowers which insects love, and the fleshy leaves have a bitter taste - best blanched before adding to a salad! The Ivy-leaved toadflax (Cymbalaria muralis) arrived from the Mediterranean region in about 1640. It has tiny leaves and small, lilac and yellow, snapdragon, flowers. It will pour down a sunny wall with fine stems up to 3 feet long, or cluster at the top, covering the coping stones with a mat of bright flowers. Happily co-habiting is another introduced plant that works equally hard for a living; Corydalis lutea - the Yellow Fumitory - has clusters of small, yellow, tubular flowers above beautiful ferny leaves. It is equally at home clinging to gaps in the mortar, or growing in showy mounds at ground level.

Campanula poscharskyana

In shady, damp areas, the cracks and crevices may be filled with exquisite, small,
native ferns, the commonest of which are; Maidenhair spleenwort (Asplenium trichomanes),
Wall rue (Asplenium ruta-muraria) and the Rusty-back fern (Asplenium ceterach).
Rosie and I discovered all three growing on a wall in our garden! Back on the warm dry surfaces,
lichens (curious fungi growing with an algae) flourish - the orange plaques of various
Caloplacas and Xanthoria, and the grey crusts of Solemsopsora and Aspicilia….So there!
But finding lichen is very good news; they are sure indicators of clean air.

Campanula portenschlagiana

There is one Mediterranean visitant which refuses to leave, even when asked.
Helxine soleirolii - 'Mind your own Business'- could be, possibly, just
about, tolerable, if it kept its soggy, mossy drifts to
walls, or, even better, around the back of places
behind the pipes. But it has a pernicious
tendency to invade lawns, strangle the grass,
and set up a nasty, spongy home for itself.
Nothing will kill it. Not even flame-throwers.
And people, unwittingly, still buy little pots of
the creepy thing in garden centres. Just so
they can spread its infernal contagion!

Chapter Ten

WORLEBURY AND THE WOODS

Entrance to the woods, Eastcombe Road

From Birnbeck, along South and Cecil Roads to Eastcombe Gardens and Wood Lane, there are about eight pathways into the Woods. Some are steeply stepped such as from Camp Road, or at the top of Arundell Road. Others meander into the trees, as in Eastcombe Road and Wood Lane. Many of the early houses, whose gardens backed onto the woods, had their own gateways through a rear stone wall. That wall was built around 1812 when the Lord of the Manor, John Pigott, enclosed the land in Weston-super-Mare. The villagers' sheep and cattle were forced from their grazing land and Pigott proceeded to develop a private "game-preserve."[44]

The Woods are so much part of Weston's setting it is difficult to imagine the town without them. Actually, you have only to look over to Brean Down and Sand Point to get a clear picture of how things might have looked. There the grassy downland of the two sister promontories is maintained by grazing rabbits, sheep and cattle. It is also difficult to believe that in 1936, the Borough Council turned down the woods when they were on offer for £10,000. Some time later the Council did an about turn, but by then the price had risen to £22,500 for less land! If the war had not intervened one wonders just how much of the woods might have been left.[45] In the end the town acquired over 300 acres so that the townspeople could continue to use the woods as they had done since late Victorian times, when the Smyth-Pigotts opened them up to the public.

[44] It is said that a later Lord of the Manor, John Hugh Smyth-Pigott, got the idea for a wooded estate when he visited Sir Walter Scott in Scotland, returning enthused with the writer's love of trees. The tale is that Smyth-Pigott then enlisted local children to plant acorns and seedlings. After several attempts the woods were established. By the early 1900s the trees were mainly conifers and red squirrels were abundant, feeding on the pine cones. During the First World War the woodland was practically clear-felled and since then a rather random mix of native and alien tree species has become established, grey squirrels along with them, displacing their red cousins. Only recently has a woodland management plan been put into action.

[45] In the 1950s I remember seeing advertising boards which the development company erected near the water-tower, offering land for building on the northern slopes of the hill. The houses only got as far as Cliff Road, but it was a near thing.

Ashcombe Wood

Worlebury Hill-fort in Winter

Only a small proportion of the walkers in the woods get there by the southern hillside paths. Most park their cars on the wide stony road which runs from Worlebury Hill Road to the water-tower, and set off from there. During the war large numbers of American military vehicles were parked here under tree cover. The water-tower[46] provides a convenient landmark; it has been standing since 1924 as a reservoir for the hillside town and nearly all the woodland paths meet below it.

The two paths that run off to the south-east and south-west arrive at Wood Lane and Arundell Road respectively. The former then passes on eastwards through an area called Ashcombe Wood, which is designated as 'ancient woodland'. When sheep grazed the hill it was protected by an encircling wall. There is an abandoned quarry here which feels like a secret place. A splendid, mature oak stands guard at its entrance. At one time plays were performed in the wooded amphitheatre of the quarry.

[46] *The main Weston reservoir is at the top of Montpelier. The initial water supply for the town was from an energetic spring in Ashcombe - the Waterworks still resides there, at the bottom of Ashcombe Park. The original spring is no longer used, and most of Weston's water now comes from the Mendips.*

The Worlebury Hill-fort

'The Ancient British Encampment'

Over the past thirty years the fort ramparts have been almost overwhelmed by woodland growth, masking its visual impact, power, and strategic importance. The hill was probably first fortified during the Late Iron Age (after 300 BC - a particularly hostile period), and occupied by the Dobunni people whose range extended from Gloucester. Any ship's captain sailing the Severn Sea would have noticed the Worlebury promontory and its natural defences. Worlebury also had the advantages of surrounding pasture and protective marshland.

The hill-fort occupies the western end of Worle Hill. The northern side had protective cliffs, but to the south, east and west, massive dry stone walls and ditches were constructed. The walls had a complex structure of buttressing and probably rose to over 10m. (30ft.) in height with a base width of about the same. The most vulnerable area was the eastern approach - the relatively flat hilltop - and here a deep ditch was dug with two enormous defensive walls and a further five ditches. The main entrance is on the southern flank where the walls turned inwards to form a defensible passageway. There were smaller gateways at the north-east corner and in the west - the latter may have been the route to fresh water in Spring Cove (the ancient spring was lost in a landslip some years after the toll road was constructed). There are two further eastern ditches which run in parallel northwards - they probably demarcate a corralled area for sheep and cattle.

Within the fort enclosure (about 10 acres) are a large number of pits left open since they were first excavated in 1851. Most of these would have been used for storage; barley, wheat and oat grain were discovered. Others pits which were probably located inside the iron-age houses, revealed small personal items such as rings and earthenware fragments. The houses themselves were of varying size - the largest, 15m (50ft.) in diameter, was probably the headman's - with dry stone walls and conical thatched roofs.

It seems that life at the hill-fort came to a tragic end with attack and massacre. The original excavation came upon the remains of about eighteen individuals, ten of whom showed signs of wounding. One pit contained three bodies, and one skull had been "gashed with seven sword cuts." There was evidence of burning on the entrance walls. Spearheads and pikes were found. Just who the enemy was remains a mystery. It was unlikely to be the Romans, massacre was not their style and they usually took slaves. It's more likely it was another iron-age tribe, attacking sometime before the Romans arrived in Britain.

Moving west from the water-tower, the stony road proceeds along the crest of the hill and past a curious pile of stones called Peak Wina.[47] Within a few hundred yards the path divides. To the right it continues down to Birnbeck and the Toll Road and straight ahead leads to the Hill-fort or what always used to be called "The Ancient British Encampment." The modern path (there was originally a narrow Victorian one) has been cut indiscriminately through the eastern rampart walls (this is a scheduled Ancient Monument), and tree growth has so enshrouded the whole site it is difficult to understand just how important this place was. Moving through the camp there are pits to either side of the path with ferns growing on their walls. The northern cliff edge looks out over Sand Bay. At one time, the pathway ended at the western extremity with a view of Steep Holm. That too has disappeared behind the vigorous growth of ash and Holm oak. The steps continue on down, past the former Coast Guard lodge, to Camp Road and St. Joseph's Church.

Bluebells, Weston Wood

[47] *Peak Wina (or Picwinner) was a cairn created by fishermen who tossed a stone onto the pile for good fortune. As they passed they called out " Peak Wina, Peak Wina, Pick me a good dinner." 'Wina' may have been St. Winna, Bishop of Wessex in 660 AD.*

Back at the water-tower, the northerly path, which has been etched out of the hillside, descends through beech woodland, to the Kewstoke end of the Toll Road. The dense leaf canopy suppresses the undergrowth here and you can see a long way between the trees. Many big trees were blown down during the 1989 hurricane and their horizontal corpses with huge root balls lie stricken on the woodland floor. Where the pathway ends, just above the Toll Road,[48] there is a group of Sweet chestnut trees. In a hot summer the prickly chestnuts will be scattered about - enough for you and the squirrels. In spring, this part of the woods will be full of "the mist of bluebells."

The eastward road from the water-tower runs along the crest of the hill. Before the 1930-50s housing, this stony road started and ended at the small lodge where Smyth-Pigott's woodsman lived (this later became 'the Old Lodge;' a post-office grocery shop and tea-room complete with lumpy tennis court). It is rendered and castellated- the other wood-lodge, at the Kewstoke Toll Road entrance, was built in a similar style. The woods cover the hillside slopes into Sand Bay and, amongst the trees, there is evidence of prehistoric field systems and mining for zinc and lead.[49] Here too, the woodland floor is covered with bluebells in springtime.

From the woodsman's lodge to the Worlebury Golf Course, the land, now occupied by houses, was taken up with horticulture and market gardens.[50]

[48] The Kewstoke Toll Road followed an old path-line from Weston to Kewstoke, and was built by John Hugh Smyth-Pigott in 1848 as a scenic extension to his estate. It is a beautiful road, running the northern circumference of the hill with Sand Bay glittering between the trees. With the development of Worle and Wick St. Lawrence it is in danger of becoming too busy - even with the toll.

[49] This lumpy land of old mine workings is called 'gruffy ground' locally. Other areas of Worlebury have been similarly worked. German miners first arrived here in 1566 but there is evidence that mining had been going on here some time before that. The Romans had been busy on the Mendips. Mining for zinc was still going on in 1829, and for lead as late as 1845. Yellow ochre was still being taken from the south slopes in the 1920s!

[50] Much of the sunny slopes of Worlebury, from Milton into Worle, was occupied by market gardens of varying size. They supplied Weston with its vegetables, fruit and flowers for over a hundred years, right up to the 1960s. See The Good Earth by Gillian Moore.

There are still footpaths which track across old small-holding fieldways to Monks Hill. A last bit of undeveloped land, off Woodspring Avenue, has been set aside for a new school and work is due to begin at the time of writing. Opposite the future school entrance are Monks Steps[51] which lead down a ravine (now a wooded coombe) and across the lower part of Monks Hill. The route then descends a stepped wall, and on down through woodland to come out opposite St. Paul's Church in Kewstoke. Monks Hill is one of the steepest in the district with a gradient of 1:4.

[51] *It is likely that Monks' Steps were a pathway from Milton hamlet to its parish church in Kewstoke. They were once known as the Pass of St. Kew. St. Kew was a hermit of local legend who lived in a rocky cell at the top of the ravine. The Steps are now in the care of The National Trust. Monks Hill is seriously steep and riding up it by bike was a challenge. I once got to the top, from Kewstoke, without stopping, only to find that I had bent my new alloy handlebars. At other times people would overtake me at walking pace as I sweated away in low gear. It was never worth it.*

Worlebury Golf Course inhabits much of the eastern hilltop, overlooked by a parade of verandad houses along Worlebury Hill Road delineating its southern boundary. Public footpaths cross the golf course at various points, some lead into Worle, others into Kewstoke. Worlebury Hill Road itself ends dramatically at a prominent Weston landmark - The Observatory. This white tower stands like a huge chess piece at the eastern limit of the hill. It started life as a windmill in the 18th century and in 1889 the mill tower was converted into an observatory and tea-room. Since then it has lost its look-out cupola and is now part of a private house. Worlebury Hill Road continues as a stony track down into Worle. The footpath around the Observatory looks down into Worle Quarry, and the view across Wick St. Lawrence and North Worle reveals the relentless growth of the town. Weston appears stalled upon a bluff, poised to pour forward into cowering Kewstoke and Sand Bay.

The Observatory, Worlebury Hill

Chapter Eleven

THE PARKS

Weston-super-Mare's early master-builders had definite ideas about the place into which they were pouring their energy and their money. They needed to preserve the town's salubrity, its health-giving ozone. Views and perspectives were important, but as well as the sands and the sea, the 'genteel visitors' expected sheltered parks and shrubberies in which to rest and recuperate.

Grove Park

Many of the private estates incorporated
a parkland area, and many of these still exist.
A good number are in want of care and
attention but some, Eastfield Park for example, are
beautifully maintained. In 1856, one of the largest open
spaces acquired for the town was Ashcombe Cemetery, and
from the start it was conceived as a garden. During the
1870 - 80s the economy stalled somewhat, and as a result land was released by
developers and taken up by the town. In this way Prince Consort Gardens (described
in 'The Hillside' chapter) and Grove Park became public open space, and a donation of
land brought about the landscaping of Clarence Park. The land for Ashcombe Park was
gradually accumulated over some fifty years before it was formally opened in 1902.

GROVE PARK

In as much as it was the Smyth-Pigott 'pleasure grounds,'
The Grove was Weston's first designed open space.
Grove House started out as a cottage by the sea and
was gradually enlarged during the 19th century.
The land around the house was landscaped with terraces, shrubs and picturesque walks.
In the upper park J.H. Smyth-Pigott built an observatory tower,[52] and small quarries
were turned into ponds and waterfalls.

[52]*I remember the observatory, which was there when I roamed Grove Park in the 1940s. It was a few yards
to the right of the park entrance at the top of Grove Lane. The 20 ft. tower was built of stone with steps spiralling
around the outside, to reach a circular platform whose centre was missing. Looking down from the top, the floor of the
tower was full of branches, rubbish and leaves. It was a magnet for children and, in the end, one of us fell
off and broke an arm. So the poor old observatory was blamed and pulled down.*

[53]*Mind you these loos are locally famous and well cared for, the attendants having received
Best Kept' awards for their work. It's just that they are in the wrong place.*

After the Smyth-Pigotts had handed The Grove over to the town in 1891 it was carefully landscaped, and the wonderful cast-iron Bandstand (by the Hills Brothers' Sun Foundry) erected. The park's essential topography has remained much the same since that time. Peculiar things have happened though. Such as putting the public toilets[53] (in the 1960s) smack up against the main entrance - an act of brain-numbing philistinism.

The Civic Society wall, railings and pillarshave succeeded in reclaiming some dignity and obscuring the car-park. The Grove House was bombed during 1942 and what remains is its coach house with a modern extension. To the right of the stable door, a mulberry tree drops fruit in late summer, and in June the building is fronted by a spectacular bank of Nevada roses - huge creamy-white scented flowers in wonderful profusion. From here, you can step down into a walled garden, which may have been part of the original terracing to Grove Cottage. The garden, now dedicated to Jill Dando,[54] had an exciting makeover by the BBC Ground Force team in July 2001. Look out for the small tile painting of forget-me-nots by Rosie Smith.

The upper and lower parks have distinct personalities. The lower is rather formal; the bandstand, the pond and the war memorial giving it a precise shape. But as you ascend the steps to the 'top of the park' the tree canopy thickens and it can be a bit spooky. This used to be a rather wild place (in the best sense), but it has been tidied up and there's a small playground close to where the ruined observatory used to stand. In the 'bottom of the park' look for railings high in the oak tree to the right of the south-west entrance - they arrived there by way of bomb blast in 1941. A short distance from the same entrance is a pergola passageway of wisteria and laburnum whose fragrance can be intoxicating in early summer. It leads to a scented garden for the blind. And there are still newts in the rockery ponds.

[54]Jill Dando was shot dead on the doorstep of her London home in April 1999.
She was born and educated in Weston, and began her career as a journalist on the Weston Mercury.
She became hugely popular as a BBC television broadcaster,
and was a passionate advocate for her home town.

ASHCOMBE PARK

Ashcombe Park's 36 acres makes it the largest of Weston's parks. During the 19th century various attempts to develop it had been resisted by the Weston Local Board. It was felt that the Ashcombe hillside protected the Ashcombe spring from contamination - Weston's most important water source at that time. By virtue of being laid out on the side of a hill, Ashcombe, like Grove Park, has a satisfying mix of copses, coombes and sunlit slopes. The bowling greens, close by the Milton Road entrance, have a superb open pavilion (it started life on the promenade, close to Claremont Crescent), although the same can't be said for the modern attachment. From the main entrance runs an avenue of lime trees which takes you to the upper park with its wooden shelter and park-keeper's lodge. The western part of the park, which runs down alongside Ashcombe Park Road, is great for tobogganing. Should it ever manage to snow.[55]

[55] *Sam, my son, has always claimed that by living in Weston-super-Mare, he had had a childhood "seriously deprived of snow." And it's true! My own childhood seems to have been the opposite somehow. I lived on Worlebury, and Dad's Austin 16 was always getting stuck in the snow on Milton Hill.*

The Cemetery, looking to Christ Church and the sea

Entering through the north-east gate, you step down into the park, and are straightaway insulated from the traffic busying along Upper Bristol Road. There's a cafe here, where you can sit outside and gaze across the grassy slopes in summer. Following the path on down, you arrive at three tennis courts - the most sheltered and pleasant in all Weston. Like so many of the town's courts, they are poorly maintained and, because of that, under-used. Passing through a Horse chestnut grove, you arrive at a wooden ticket-hut and an excellent Pitch and Putt course. There are also some unplayable lawn tennis courts, where balls have been known to bounce back across the net of their own accord.

Ashcombe Cemetery

The original lay-out in 1856 was influenced by the Garden Cemetery movement and
was conceived as a home for rare trees, ferns and other plants. At one time the main
entrance from Lower Bristol Road led down to two small Gothic chapels, mirror images
of one another, built in the Villa Rosa limestone. For some unfathomable reason the eastern
chapel was demolished, and this has left its sibling standing alone and incomplete,
a bereaved twin. The upper gates are watched over by a pretty Gothic lodge.
The entrance lodge to the Milton Road gates originally headed the carriageway to
Ashcombe House (now lost, but which stood at the top of The Drive), which served
as the local Maternity Hospital up to 1985.

During summer the cemetery
becomes a hillside meadow.
Benign neglect favours the long grass,
rose garlic and field butterflies. In
June there is a heady scent of lime
tree blossom accompanied by an
intense thrumming of inebriated
bees. The paths dive and weave
between the graves, with glimpses
of Christ Church in the middle
distance, and tucked down on the
sheltered western border there
is a small military cemetery with
headstones to British, German
and Polish war dead.
It's a comforting place.

CLARENCE PARK

In 1882, Clarence Park arrived by way of a donation of land by Rebecca Davies
in memory of her husband William Henry. The move wasn't entirely altruistic -
it encouraged further building in the southern areas of the town in the 1880s,
and W. Henry Davies had been an energetic developer. Rebecca was subsequently
a bit miffed when the town was slow to lay out the park. So she died two days before
the proposed formal opening. For some reason, the park is named after Albert,
Duke of Clarence.

Lodge, Clarence Park, with Howard's bike

The park is divided into east and west by Walliscote Road, each having its own character. Clarence Park East has been laid out fairly formally with a Gothic Lodge, a pond with a fountain, shrubberies, trees and walks. The bowling club and its greens reside in the southern part, and the setting is beautiful, except for the recent brick club-house extension which is turgid and heavy handed - similar to the affliction that has happened in Ashcombe Park. Why couldn't it have taken a cue from the engaging Victorian kiosk and shelter in the middle of the park? The large houses along Beach Road, together with the shelter planting of Holm oaks down the western boundary, shield the park from the onshore breezes. This part is relaxed and grassy, comfortable and sheltered in summer.

Clarence Park East has always been used for sport, and until 1996 was the home of the Weston Cricket Festival,[56] held every August. The cricket pavilion still stands, lonely now, under the pines. The cricket square, for all those years defended by wooden fencing, has now surrendered to hockey and football.

[56] *The Weston-super-Mare County Cricket Festival was a wonderful annual occasion that had taken place in*
Clarence Park since 1914, only being interrupted by the two world wars.
It was one of those fixed times in the year when you might run into old friends.
Originally it took in three Somerset County Cricket matches over eleven days,
but in later years shrank to one four day match and a Sunday game. Despite intense efforts by
local supporters there was little commitment from Somerset C.C.C. to support the event,
and so Weston festival cricket died.
"Ah, Botham, Richards and Garner of long ago...."

See Rosie Smith's Clarence Park tile panel at the Winter Gardens, which shows Somerset
batting against Worcestershire on August 8th 1991.
The time is 11.10am, it's a warm sunny morning on the final day and Somerset are 27 for no wicket.
Jimmy Cook is facing the bowler Neal Radford with Peter Roebuck backing up at the Town End.
I know because I was there.

Chapter Twelve

KEWSTOKE AND SAND BAY

On the other side of Worlebury Hill is Weston's secret seaside. Here the wooded slopes reach the Sand Bay shoreline, interrupted only by the Kewstoke Toll Road passing, unseen, beneath the trees. In Spring this hillside is alight with wild flowers and unfolding ferns, sunlight streaming through the fresh green canopy of emerging leaves. Coming down out of the woods from the Water Tower, the bridle path ends at the Toll Road junction. Set back in the trees, close to the site of the demolished woodsman's cottage, is a cafe, complete with castellations and views to Sand Point. Across the road is the Shell Shop, full of seasidey things and milk lollies. Below the walled parapet of the Toll Road, the way to the beach folds back on itself, curving past the grounds of the Kewstoke Convalescent Home.[57] Despite being built on the scale of a Grand Hotel, and despite a stark and immaculate whiteness, this building somehow manages to remain largely unseen. Meanwhile the road continues on down to the beach between the woods and grassy verges.

The road along the Sand Bay shoreline[58] runs its whole length tucked below a sea wall or a grassy embankment. The landward side of the embankment, protected from the wind, is a profusion of flowers. When Rosie and I walked along Beach Road in early May, amongst the high grass were bright yellow charlock and creeping buttercups and the purple flowers of clary and bush vetch. And just a few more we couldn't name. Sand Bay beach has more than its share of flotsam and jetsam. If it wasn't for plastic, its untidiness would be a pleasure. All the same it's great for beachcombing - my brothers and I once built a toboggan from wood garnered from the bay. Our father went one better and made a kitchen cupboard.

[57] *Built in the early 1930s the home has retained its dramatic Mediterranean character. Inside it is even more atmospheric, for with high windows and sweeping staircases, it evokes the stage set of a Noel Coward play.*

[58] *In the 1970s the Sand Bay sea defences were under threat with the consequent risk of flooding on the Kewstoke levels between Worlebury and Sand Point. Vast quantities of gravel were dredged from the Bristol Channel and laid out along Sand Bay, to a depth of over 10 feet in places. It was dirty stuff and made the bay unpleasant for a long time. Now the coastline has stabilised and the familiar firm sand has returned.*

Below Sand Point is an extensive field of spartina grass. Another coastal defence effort which went a bit out of control. Many attempts to limit its spread have failed, although it does seem to have slowed down a bit in recent years. The Sand Point peninsula, rising to a mere 162 feet, lacks the pomp of Brean Down, but its smaller scale gives it an intimacy its big brother doesn't have. The sea is close at hand and the rocks less forbidding. On the north side of Sand Point are the pebbled bays of Middle Hope with St. Thomas's Head close by. In the near distance is the tower of Woodspring Priory sheltered by the coastal rising. The grass is kept cropped by grazing sheep and cattle, dry stone walls mark the boundaries of old fields and all the Bristol Channel is laid out before you. In autumn the blackberries make good picking.

Sand Point and Sand Bay

Although it beckons, there is no public access to Woodspring Priory from Middle Hope, and the best route is from North Worle, along Collum Lane. As you pass Colm Farm there is a slight rise in the land, and the Priory stands invitingly at the end of the lane, which continues towards it between open meadows.

Back at the Toll Road junction, Kewstoke Road takes up the journey into the village. The road has managed to remain pleasingly narrow, with stone walls and grass verges, and the attendant risk of being pressed flat by passing cars. The character of this cosy road has changed a lot in recent years with oppressively large houses set back onto the hillside, where once horses grazed and wild flowers grew. Up above, on 'The Headlands,' the grass was kept short and tufty by a multitude of rabbits. It was a wonderful place which we, as children, seemed to have to ourselves.

Kewstoke Village

A short walk along Kewstoke Road and you arrive at St. Paul's Church, huddled at the bottom of Monks Hill. The small hall, to the west of the church, once functioned as a poor house apparently. I remember it as a Sunday School, and in the 1950s the entrance was through a small stone porch in the middle of the south wall, which opened directly onto the road. The well tended churchyard lights up in Spring with cherry blossom. The old rectory, a fine Georgian residence, sits next to the church on its west side, amongst shading trees.

Gate House with Red Valerians, Woodspring Priory, high summer

The church of St. Paul has Norman origins, and the beautiful carved doorway is from that time. It was enlarged in the 15th century, and later substantially rebuilt in the Victorian period. It was then that the wooden chalice was discovered hidden in the north wall (See special page on Woodspring Priory). Immediately across Kewstoke Road from the church is a public footpath, which runs up through a woodland garden. It leads to the boundary wall of Monks Hill, surmounted by stone steps let into the masonry. From here Monks Steps (the Pass of St. Kew) rise through, what has become, a wooded coombe, to end at Woodspring Avenue, close to Worlebury Golf Course (see footnote in Worlebury and the Woods).

Much of the land between Kewstoke Village and the sea has been taken over by caravan parks, which are eroding its pastoral atmosphere. It's a shame too, that a much-needed village hall has been incongruously built of red factory-brick and plonked in the middle of a field. Little thought having been given to the context of the old village, and the impact the hall would have on the ambience of the bay.

An older Kewstoke is still to be found - Victory Cottages, just off the top of Crooks Lane, were built in 1759 when General Wolfe defeated the French in Quebec, and the New Inn is built on the site of a much older hostelry. The Commodore, on Beach Road, grew up from a row of fishermen's cottages. And, perhaps most famously of all, there is Electron House on Kewstoke Road, where Mr. J. Dando serviced Electron Batteries between the wars!

Elderberries

Woodspring Priory

Three of the four knights, who murdered Thomas A Becket in 1170, were West countrymen. One, Reginald Fitz Urse, owned Woodspring (then called 'Worspring') which through marriage eventually passed to a wealthy landowner; William de Courtenay. In the early 13th century William built a chapel at Worspring dedicated to "the blessed martyr Thomas," and soon after he asked the Bishop of Bath if he could establish an Augustinian Priory "to hasten the salvation" of himself and his family. All of Thomas's assassins got off pretty lightly and expressed little contrition for what they had done, so it is uncertain if the priory was an act of penance. In 1849, during repairs to the north wall of Kewstoke Church, a small wooden vessel was found in an 18 inch carved cavity. The bottom of the cup was stained with blood. It has been considered that this might be the blood of St. Thomas, and that the sacred relic was hidden by priory canons at the time of the Dissolution of the Monasteries in 1536. The priory seal shows the head of the saint being attacked with a sword, a chalice on a ledge close at hand.

At its inception Worspring Priory was not well off, but in the 15th century things looked up, and many of the buildings we can see today were constructed. These are: the barn, the infirmary, as well as the priory church and tower (Somerset Perpendicular), which replaced the original de Courtenay chapel. For a century or so the canons did pretty well until the Reformation in 1534 when Prior Tormenton refused to acknowledge Henry VIII's supremacy. The Prior swiftly sold off the priory assets and the community was duly 'suppressed' in 1536.

Over the years it was used as a family residence and bits of the priory buildings were knocked down and reused in other structures. At the end of the 17th century the priory was acquired by the Smyth-Pigotts who built the farmhouse. It was around this time that 'Worspring' became 'Woodspring' - it is not known why. In the late 1800s it had a short career as a golf course, but then reverted to a family farm once again. The estate was acquired by the National Trust in 1968, with the priory buildings passing into the care of the Landmark Trust soon after.

Chapter Thirteen

THE VILLAGES

Approaching Uphill, along The West Mendip Way

Perusing an 1809 Ordnance Survey map, Weston-super-Mare barely registers any more significance than the neighbouring hamlets of Ashcombe and Milton. It does have a small parish church, albeit a trifle neglected, but Weston village looks to Worle for most of its needs, and especially its ale. The map shows the main route to Uphill to be along the beach, where the sand is flat and firm - the marshy landward track often becoming impassable. The road to Worle is half way up the Worlebury hillside - following the present day line of the Lower and Upper Bristol Roads - again to avoid vulnerable low lying land, susceptible to flood.

UPHILL

The easiest way to Uphill, from Weston, is still along the sands. The small unroofed church of St. Nicholas is poised on its quarried cliff above the Axe, a dramatic pause to the Mendips, which then close with Brean Down and Steep Holm. The church[59] is visible for miles around, from the sea and the surrounding country, and for centuries has served as an important landmark. It must have been particularly so when it used to be whitewashed - as it is today when floodlit, glowing by night at the southern end of Weston Bay.

The 18th century poet William Lisle Bowles, who so inspired Samuel T. Coleridge, spent much of his childhood in Uphill - his father was Rector from 1769 to 1786 and he describes his arrival in the village in a relaxed and conversational verse;

> *My father came, the pastor of this church*
> *That crowns the high hill crest above the sea;*
> *When, as the wheels went slow, and the still night*
> *Seemed listening, a low murmer met the ear,*
> *Not of the winds: my mother softly said,*
> *Listen! it is the sea!*   (from the poem Banwell Hill)

Little of Bowles' Uphill remains - although you can still hear the sea. His father's old church still looks out over the Severn Sea, and a step back to the east is the stump of a windmill converted into a look-out tower. Below the north side of the hill, in Uphill Way, are The Ship and The Dolphin, inns whose names go back to the 18th century at least, and are a reminder of the village's maritime provenance. Uphill had probably been a port[60] since Roman times, shipping out lead from the Mendip mines. Access to Welsh coal was one of the reasons that the first local brickyards were here - and there was a regular packet service to Wales and to Ireland.

---

[59] *There is a story that it was first decided to build the church in the valley, but by night, after each day's labour, the building materials mysteriously found their way to the top of the hill. It was believed that St. Nicholas, patron saint of seafarers, had taken a hand. So the church ended up on the hill!*

[60] *A Roman road has been traced from Uphill to Salisbury (Old Sarum). The Uphill port records were probably lost in the Bristol Riots, but it is known that in 1731 the 'Jesse' from South Carolina docked. Her cargo is not known.*

Today the muddy banks of the Axe have a busy clutter of sailing boats waiting for the next high tide. To the left of the entrance to the boat yard is the closing Marker Post for the West Mendip Way, which runs from Wells to Uphill - or vice-versa if you're walking eastwards! The beach road (Links Road) runs past the boatyard to the remoter holes of the Weston golf course and Slimeridge Farm (new version), ending at the southern extremity of the sand-dunes and a Second World War blockhouse.

The donkey field, Uphill

Nowadays the village struggles to maintain its physical independence from Weston, and has been made more vulnerable by the General Hospital arriving on the south-east border. The northern borders seem more secure, with Uphill Manor[61] land, woods owned by the Woodland Trust, and Uphill Castle Cricket Club. Entering the village from Uphill Road North there is still a sense of separation, with the shade cast by high trees, the castellated wall of the Manor estate watched over by a Gothic gate-lodge. The bosky atmosphere is relieved by a small open pasture known as 'the donkey field' - although there have been no donkeys here for quite a while. In spring and summer this is Uphill's treasured place - an enchanting meadow of bluebells and cowslips. Old Church Road curves round the southern perimeter of the field, wanders on between a comfortable assortment of houses and cottages and ends bridging The Great Uphill Rhyne (which is pretending to be a stream). Between here and the sea are a number of small pre and post-war housing estates, a scatter of Victorian terraces and Coastguard cottages.

---

[61] *Known locally as Uphill Castle. The original house was built in 1805 but on being sold to Thomas Tutton-Knyfton in 1853 was enlarged in the Victorian High Gothic style. With the recent sale of the estate the new owners have restored the Augustus Pugin wallpapers - reprinted from the original blocks. The Castle now serves as a guest house.*

The Airfield

Weston has been described as "a town with a hole in the middle." The 'hole' is Weston Airfield, which was planned and approved by the local council in the early 1930s. In 1936 the Hutton Moor was drained and layed out with an airport terminal and a 14,000 sq. ft. hangar. The terminal building had started life as a First World War hospital, and the control tower top was a redundant cab shelter from the sea-front! The facilities were leased to Western Airways who flew DeHavilland aircraft between Weston and Cardiff. Later on they established a Weston-Bristol-Birmingham-Manchester service.

The airport was poised for expansion when the Second World War intervened. Western Airways then became involved with the RAF, and RAF Locking opened as a school of technical training close by. In 1939 the airfield was requisitioned by the Government. Factories, building and repairing aircraft such as the Bristol Beaufighter and Avro Anson, opened on the fringes of the airfield. Weston had a very busy war indeed.

After the war there were, briefly, plans to build the huge Bristol Brabazon at Weston but the runway could not be upgraded. In 1948 the Weston-Cardiff run was reinstituted with fares of £1.12p return and a journey time of about 8 minutes. Commercial flying faded away in the 1950s, but gliding and other leisure flying continued into the 1980s. Bristol helicopters were built in Oldmixon from the 1950s. The factory was taken over by Westlands in 1961 and has followed a difficult course since then. The International Helicopter Museum was established in 1974 by local enthusiasts and in 1988 moved onto land close to the original terminal buildings. These were partly demolished in 2000, although at the time of writing, the cab shelter control tower was still there, tottering on the eastern airport rim. RAF Locking closed in the same year.

It is only a generation or so ago Worle, especially on the hillside, stood clear of
Weston. From the Windsor Castle pub, the main road used to curve up through the
market gardens of Milton Hill to Worlebury, while Spring Hill, a narrow country lane
with high hedges of hawthorn and woodbine, tipped up and down into Worle village.
Today the top of Spring Hill has become a cul-de-sac, and houses have filled the nursery
slopes. Some of the old village atmosphere returns as we approach St. Martin's church,
from Weston, along Church Road. Here the village school occupies what was originally
a Monastic Barn.[62] Although little of the medieval building remains, in its proportions
and scale the spirit of the old barn survives somehow. The buttresses, along the
pavement on Church Road, appear to have belonged to the original north wall,
and tie in with John Rutter's small etching in his book on north-west Somerset.

Church Road, Worle

The Round House

Just to the east of
St. Martin's, the road narrows
and turns as it enters the remains of the
old village. The houses and cottages here press up
against each other - a mixture of the grand and the previously humble -
with the roads making themselves awkward in the way they fold back on
each other. The Round House, at the top of Lawrence Road, squeezes into
the 90 degree angle of criss-crossing roads with no pavements. At the southern end
of Ebdon Road, Magnolia Cottage (a big cottage!) is the last representative of a
thatched roof in the village.

[62]*The barn was apparently owned by Woodspring Priory and in 1829 John Rutter described the ruin as being of*
'superior masonry'. When the old barn became a school Jonathan Ellwell wrote;

Where once was heaped the produce of the soil,
The lamp of learning is kept trimmed with oil;
Where vagrant urchins loitering near the door,
Heard sounds suggestive of the threshing floor

Directly opposite the church an old footpath cuts north, through the new houses and bungalows, to the steep, wooded hillside below the Observatory. The woodland, enclosed by stone walls and with large numbers of Scots pine and Holm oak, recalls the original coniferous planting carried out by John Hugh Smyth-Pigott in the 1820s. The path itself (Balaam Walk) is constrained by the same stone walls but eventually opens out on to a bridleway. This continues up and along the hill to join a footpath which then journeys on into Kewstoke.

St. Martin's was founded in the early 12th century and underwent a major restoration in 1870. One especially poignant tale about the church is that in 1348, the year of the Black Death, four vicars were appointed to its ministry. As each new priest arrived, so he succumbed to the plague, only to be succeeded by another brave man. With their close contact with the sick, they must have known that they would almost certainly die.

St. Martin's is comfortable in its hillside setting. It sits amongst trees and enjoys a south facing churchyard which steps down into a lower cemetery. This, baffingly, runs out into a bleak tarmacadam car park. The horrible, beige-brick health centre then completes the disruption of a becoming vista by disconnecting the village high street from its church.

Worle[63] High Street is a congested road, which has just managed to hold on to a few of its Victorian terraced houses. Primrose House (No.188), is a lonely survivor of the 'three windows up, two windows down and a door in the middle' sort of cottage, that once filled the High Street. You can still see the small turret of the departed Imperial Laundry (it was a brewery before that). The Woodspring (formerly the New Inn) survives from days when High Street was called Lower Street, and Weston was just a gleam in the eyes of Messrs Parsley and Cox.

[63]*In his book 'The Somerset Coast' in 1909, Charles Harper describes Worle ("Wurle") as*
"a detestable village of vulgar and poverty-stricken shops and out-at-elbows cottages, a blot on its surroundings."
Which seems a bit harsh! John Rutter, eighty years earlier, had waxed lyrical;
"pleasantly situated on the south east declivity of the hill.....it bears a cheerful character and the dwellings have generally an appearance of neatness and comfort."

Looking west from the top of Hutton Court Tower

Along the old Uphill to Banwell Road, lie a number of hamlets and villages occupying the lower northern slopes of West Mendip. From west to east, they are; Old Mixon, Hutton, Elborough and Knightcott. Of these, only Hutton has managed to resist assimilation, protected by the Airfield (so far) to the north. Elborough, with the demolition of the large aircraft engineering works and an explosion of house building, now defies its definition as a hamlet. Along with Knightcott, it is being absorbed into the outer fringes of Banwell. For all that, it's good to have the view of Crooks Peak back again, beyond Christon Hill.

Summer house ruin, Hutton Court

Hutton is an ancient village dating
from beyond Domesday. The main road ('The Street' to locals), which runs from west to
east has many traditional Somerset farmhouses - though the farms and their orchards are
long gone. Some of these houses go back to the 15th century. A lot of post-war housing
has gone up north of Main Road, but it has left the heart of the village relatively untouched.
The gravitational centre of Hutton is the great Horse chestnut tree, which stands opposite
the school at the entrance to Church Lane. From here the road continues up and out of
the village towards Canada Coombe, while Church Lane describes a semi-circular route
to the south and west, past the Old Rectory, Hutton Court and St. Mary's Church.

St. Mary's was completely rebuilt in the 15th century, but a church has stood here
from the 13th century at least. It is another beautiful example of the Somerset
Perpendicular style. The Victorians did a bit of damage by removing a "fine southern
porch" when they added a south aisle, but the church has an indefinable tranquillity,
surrounded by meadows and woods. Next door (to the east) stands Hutton Court which
has been home to various families as far back as the 13th century, although it seems likely
the present building, with its low tower and hall, was built at about the same time as the
church. In the Court gardens, set back from the house, is a ruined summer house in a
perfect state of picturesque decay, while a small doorway, in the south east corner of the
graveyard, links the manor house to its church. The Court's tower was a defensive

structure to which the family could retreat if under threat. Even the stairway twists in a clockwise direction so that the right sword arm could be used without exposing the body.

Above Hutton, and to the south-east, runs Canada Coombe[64] which follows a crooked groove, part darkly wooded, to the top of Hutton Hill, passing through the small settlements of Lower and Upper Canada. From here there are pathways taking you to the summit of Christon Hill and linking up with the West Mendip Way.[65]

LOCKING

In 1907 Knight described Locking as "a beautiful little village," with the road sloping gently past the old manor house, overshadowed by tall elms. The elms have died, although they survive here and there disguised as hedges, waiting patiently for the Dutch elm disease to make its final departure. They are remembered in the name Elm Tree Road. But Locking has not been kindly served by the 20th century. The setting of St. Augustine's Church was felt to be especially lovely, but a clutter of recent housing has obscured that. The Locking Moor Road, widened to accommodate the airport and RAF Locking, isolated the outer farms and distorted the village's centrality. RAF Locking became a small town in itself and, now it has closed, this whole area of the Northmarsh is likely to be taken up by housing.

Locking Manor, situated at the elbow of Elm Tree Close under a great Holm oak, may go back to the time of Elizabeth I but has undergone extensive rebuilding. The huge stones in the driveway were thought to have been brought there by "bullock wagons from the top of Mendip" where they had comprised part of a stone circle. Some now say that they are just a folly.

[64] *Where the name Canada Coombe came from is something of a mystery. It may be linked to the unification of Canada in 1867 when Upper and Lower Canada became Ontario and Quebec. But F.A. Knight only refers to Hutton Coombe in 1902, but does go on to mention Upper Canada Farm.*

[65] *The West Mendip Way was devised and waymarked by local Rotary Clubs to celebrate Queen Elizabeth's Jubilee in 1977. The Way was opened in May 1979. It is a wonderful walk of about 30 miles - especially westwards, towards the sea. See Andrew Eddy's 'The West Mendip Way.'*

*Locking, from the Hutton
to Banwell Road*

Looking across to Locking, from the Hutton to Banwell Road, St. Augustine's sits on
a low hill, above Church Farm, amongst sheltering limes. Entering the village from the
Hutton side, some of the old atmosphere is recaptured in the tiny coombe called The
Bury, which ends in a hill-start challenge at the top of the ridge. The view from the
church, across the meadows to the wooded slopes of Hutton Hill and the Mendips,
can't have changed much from when Knight was writing, a hundred years ago.

EPILOGUE

At night with the dog running on ahead,
Not quite night, for the sun on the ledge of Wales
Waits in its heat along the red hills.
From the wood-path the sea shows through the trees
And after the hot day the hill exhales its heat.
Everything I touch is thick with smells.

BIBLIOGRAPHY

Abram, Lawrence, 1974, Uphill and its Old Church
Arkwright Society, 1976 - 81, Local History Trails 1 - 5
Austin, Brian, Tales of Old Weston, 1992/1993, Vols. 1 and 2
Bailey, John, 1986, Weston-super-Mare. Look back with Laughter
Barrett, J. H. 1978, A History of Maritime Forts in the Bristol Channel
Beisly, Philip, 1979, The Romantic Poets in the West Country
Beisly, Philip, 1988, Weston-super-Mare, a History and Guide
Beisly, Philip, 1996, The Northmarsh of Somerset
Bizley, Joyce, 1969, The Church of St. Martin, Worle
Brickell, Christopher, 1996, The Royal Horticultural Society A - Z Encyclopedia of Garden Plants
Broomhead, Richard, 1977, Cheddar, Cheddar Gorge, Brean Down, the Mendips
Brown, Bryan and Loosley, John, 1979, The Book of Weston-super-Mare
Crockford-Hawley, John, 1990, A History of the Parish Church of All Saints
Dare and Frampton, 1888, A History of the Weston-super-Mare New Sea Front
Dymond, Charles W. 1902, Worlebury
Eddy, Andrew, 1983, The West Mendip Way
Evans, I.O. 1962, Observer's Book of Sea and Seashore
Evans, Jane, 1980, Worlebury. The Story of the Iron Age Fort
Farr, Grahame, 1954, Somerset Harbours
Harper, C.G. 1909, The Somerset Coast
Jory, Bob, 1995, Flat Holm. Bristol Channel Island
Knight, F.A. 1902, The Sea-Board of Mendip
Lambert, David, 1998, Historic Public Parks, Weston-super-Mare
Legg, Rodney, 1983, The Steep Holm Guide
Legg, Rodney and Parsons, Tony, 1990, Steep Holm Wildlife
Mitchell, Alan, 1978, A Field Guide to the Trees of Britain and Northern Europe
Moore, Gillian M. 1999, The Good Earth
Newman, Paul, 1976, Channel Passage
Overy, John and Robert, 1927, A Short History and Guide to the Weston District
Palmer, W.R. 1924, A Century of Weston-super-Mare History
Phillips, Roger, 1980, Grasses, Ferns, Mosses and Lichens of Great Britain and Ireland
Poole, Sharon, 1987, The Royal Potteries of Weston-super-Mare
Poole, Sharon, 1989, Around Weston-super-Mare in Old Photographs
Poole, Sharon, 1991, Weston-super-Mare in Old Photographs 1950s
Poole, Sharon, 2001, Weston-super-Mare 1950s - 1970s
Rendell, Stan and Joan, 1993, Steep Holm. The Story of a Small Island
Reader's Digest, 1981, Wild Flowers of Britain
Reader's Digest, 1984, Animals of Britain
Reader's Digest, 1984, Butterflies and other Insects of Britain
Robbin's, 1899, Robbin's Guide to Weston-super-Mare
Rutter, John, 1829, Delineations of the North Western Division of the County of Somerset
Ryall, Sue, 1999, The Peoples' Village. Memories of Kewstoke
Simons, Grahame, 1988, Western Airways
Terrell, Stan, 1993, Birnbeck Pier
Tomalin, D. J. 1974, Woodspring Priory
Weston-super-Mare Civic Society, 1988, Uphill/Hutton, Countryside Trails
Whittaker, A. and Green, G.W. 1983, Geology of the country around Weston-super-Mare
Willies, R.B. 1990, Westcliff - the Story of the School
Woodspring Museum Service, 1995, Worlebury Hill
Worrall, D. H. and Surtees, P. R. 1984, Flat Holm